1810 Naissance d'Alfred de Musset, le 11 décembre, à Paris. Napoléon 1er est empereur depuis six ans.

1819 Il commence de brillantes études au collège Henri IV.

1828-1830 Musset suit, avec peu d'assiduité, les cours de la Faculté de Médecine et de la Faculté de Droit, puis travaille quelque temps dans les bureaux d'une entreprise de chauffage. Il fréquente les milieux mondains et littéraires : il est bientôt adopté par les romantiques et fait la connaissance de Hugo et de Nodier. Il publie une ballade, *Un rêve,* et une traduction de *l'Anglais mangeur d'Opium* de Quincey (1828).

1830 Après la chute de l'Empire (1815), Louis XVIII a rétabli la royauté. Charles X lui a succédé en 1824. En 1830, éclate un mouvement révolutionnaire qui porte Louis-Philippe au pouvoir. Musset souhaite s'engager au côté des opposants, mais ressent cruellement la distance qui sépare la pensée de l'action. Il publie les *Contes d'Espagne et d'Italie,* œuvre marquée par une virtuosité un peu gratuite et connaît un échec avec sa pièce *la Nuit vénitienne.*

1832 Publication d'*Un spectacle dans un fauteuil,* composé de deux pièces de théâtre, *la Coupe et les Lèvres, A quoi rêvent les jeunes filles* et d'un poème, *Namouna.*

1833 Publication du drame *André del Sarto,* de la comédie *les Caprices de Marianne* et du poème *Rolla.* C'est alors que commence la liaison tumultueuse entre Musset et l'écrivain George Sand.

1834 Le séjour de Musset avec George Sand à Venise se passe très mal : la jeune femme tombe amoureuse du médecin qui soigne Musset — atteint d'une fièvre typhoïde —

PROFIL D'UNE ŒUVRE

Collection dirigée par Georges Décote

LORENZACCIO

MUSSET

Analyse critique

par Robert HORVILLE
Docteur ès Lettres
Professeur à l'Université de Lille III

Nouvelle édition

HATIER

Sommaire

© HATIER PARIS SEPTEMBRE 1987

ISSN 0750-2516   ISBN 2-218-01825-1

et c'est la rupture, bientôt suivie d'une réconcilation provisoire. Publication de deux comédies, *Fantasio* et *On ne badine pas avec l'amour,* ainsi que du drame historique, *Lorenzaccio.*

1835 Publication d'une comédie, *le Chandelier* et de deux poèmes, *la Nuit de Mai* et *la Nuit de Décembre.*

1836 Publication d'un poème, *la Nuit d'Août,* d'une comédie, *Il ne faut jurer de rien* et d'un roman autobiographique, *la Confession d'un Enfant du Siècle.*

1837 Publication de la comédie, *un Caprice* et du poème, *la Nuit d'Octobre.*

1838 Musset est nommé bibliothécaire au Ministère de l'Intérieur.

1840 A 30 ans, Musset, usé physiquement et moralement, est de moins en moins productif. Publication du poème, *une Soirée perdue* et édition de l'ensemble des œuvres qu'il a écrites jusqu'ici.

1841 Publication du poème patriotique, *le Rhin allemand.*

1845 Publication du conte *Mimi Pinson* et de la comédie *Il faut qu'une porte soit ouverte ou fermée.*

1847 Succès de la représentation de la comédie *Un caprice.*

1848 Une révolution renverse Louis-Philippe. Louis-Napoléon Bonaparte devient président de la République. Musset perd son poste de bibliothécaire.

1851 Première représentation de la comédie *Bettine.*

1852 Louis-Napoléon Bonaparte est proclamé empereur sous le nom de Napoléon III. Élection de Musset à l'Académie française.

1854 Il devient bibliothécaire au Ministère de l'Instruction publique.

1857 Le 2 mai, Musset meurt à Paris, emporté par une maladie de cœur, dans sa quarante-septième année.

2 | Musset et le théâtre romantique

Dès le XVIIIe siècle, des auteurs français, comme Diderot, avaient tenté d'assouplir le système dramatique classique légué par le XVIIe siècle.

Mais il faut attendre le début du XIXe siècle pour voir s'affirmer cette tendance que vient favoriser tout un faisceau d'influences. Le rôle que jouent, dans ce domaine, les théoriciens allemands est considérable. En 1814, la publication en France du *Cours de Littérature dramatique* de Schlegel est déterminante : l'auteur y oppose le romantisme chrétien et moderne au classicisme antique et païen ; il préconise le mélange des genres, réclame l'indépendance à l'égard des unités, souligne l'intérêt des contrastes, insiste sur la prépondérance du sentiment sur l'intelligence et apparaît ainsi comme l'initiateur du théâtre romantique français. Les Italiens, forts d'une riche tradition, apportent, eux aussi, leur pierre à l'édifice : Manzoni, dans la *Lettre sur les Unités* (1823), qui constitue un véritable réquisitoire contre la tragédie classique, donne aux partisans du changement des arguments précieux.

Et puis, bien sûr, il y a les œuvres. Les auteurs allemands Schiller (1759-1805) et Goethe (1749-1832) fournissent des exemples, des modèles à suivre. Mais c'est surtout le grand Shakespeare (1564-1616) qui sert de référence. Dans son œuvre traduite de l'anglais par Letourneur de 1776 à 1782, ce sont surtout son sens du drame historique, son goût pour les scènes pathétiques et son attirance pour le sombre et le terrifiant qui retiennent alors l'attention. En 1818, puis en

1828, le célèbre acteur anglais Kean fera applaudir à Paris le théâtre shakespearien et marquera de son empreinte auteurs, acteurs et spectateurs.

LES GRANDS PRINCIPES

Toutes ces influences ont donné naissance à une doctrine cohérente qui refuse dans le classicisme ce qui est rétrécissement et contrainte et dont les maîtres mots seraient donc ouverture et liberté. Ces grands principes, on les retrouve sous la plume de nombreux écrivains de l'époque, et notamment dans la préface de *Cromwell* de Victor Hugo, véritable manisfeste du théâtre romantique français.

La modernité

Il s'agit d'abord de sacrifier à la « modernité » et d'élaborer une œuvre qui ne soit pas intemporelle, mais qui convienne à une époque, qui réponde aux besoins et aux aspirations du public contemporain (« Le Romanticisme est l'art de présenter aux peuples les œuvres littéraires qui, dans l'état actuel de leurs habitudes et de leurs croyances, sont susceptibles de leur donner le plus de plaisir possible. Le Classicisme, au contraire, leur présente la littérature qui donnait le plus grand plaisir possible à leurs arrière-grands-pères », écrit Stendhal dans *Racine et Shakespeare* en 1823).

Décrire la complexité de la vie

Pour parvenir à ce but, il convient de décrire la vie dans la complexité de la réalité quotidienne (Le drame doit être « un tableau large de la vie, au lieu du tableau resserré de la catastrophe d'une intrigue », Vigny, *Lettre à Lord* XXX, 1830).
La couleur locale, la vérité historique jouent donc un grand rôle et tendent à substituer le spectacle direct au récit : « (...) le drame doit être radicalement imprégné de cette couleur du temps (...). Le poète doit feuilleter les siècles, interroger les chroniques », Hugo, préface de *Cromwell,* 1827).

Décrire la vie telle qu'elle est, c'est bien. En rendre compte dans sa totalité, en évitant de privilégier certains éléments au détriment d'autres, c'est encore mieux ; tout au moins dans l'optique romantique. En effet, reposant sur une vision globale du monde, le théâtre romantique s'oppose radicalement à la conception classique qui s'attache à la description d'une crise. Il s'agit pour les classiques d'analyser un moment significatif se déroulant dans un milieu dont le caractère neutre exclut le pittoresque et permet au spectateur de fixer toute son attention, non pas sur l'accessoire, sur l'anecdotique, mais sur le permanent, sur le fondamental ; les romantiques s'efforcent, au contraire, en prônant le mélange des tons et des genres, de montrer la complexité de l'existence, de faire ressentir les contradictions qui sont au centre même de la vie. Pour éviter de privilégier une vision unique du monde, ils n'hésitent pas, en particulier, à faire se succéder le grotesque et le sublime (« Le réel résulte de la combinaison toute naturelle de deux types, le sublime et le grotesque, qui se croisent dans le drame, comme ils se croisent dans la vie et dans la création », Hugo, préface de *Cromwell*). De même, l'auteur doit toucher le spectateur dans sa totalité ; il ne doit pas se contenter de faire appel à sa sensibilité, mais doit aussi susciter son intelligence, en faisant passer un « message » philosophique ou moral (« C'est le temps du Drame de la Pensée », Vigny, préface de *Chatterton,* 1835).

La liberté de l'art

Enfin, pour mener à bien cette tâche, la liberté de l'art est indispensable. La refuser, c'est aliéner le créateur et trahir la vie. Dans cette optique, il faut résolument rejeter la fameuse règle des trois unités classiques qui imposaient à une action concentrée de se dérouler en un seul lieu et dans les limites des vingt-quatre heures. C'est là, pour les romantiques, une solution créatrice d'invraisemblance et d'absurdité : « Quoi de plus invraisemblable et de plus absurde en effet que ce vestibule (...), lieu banal où nos tragédies ont la complaisance de venir se dérouler, où arrivent, on ne sait comment, les conspirateurs pour déclamer contre le tyran, le tyran pour déclamer contre les conspirateurs (...). L'action, encadrée de force dans les vingt-quatre heures, est aussi ridicule qu'encadrée dans le vestibule (...). Verser la même dose de temps à tous les événements ! (...) On rirait d'un cordonnier qui voudrait mettre le même soulier à tous les pieds » (Hugo, préface de *Cromwell*).

MUSSET : LE THÉÂTRE DU MAL DE VIVRE

Avec le recul, c'est certainement le théâtre de Musset qui apparaît comme le plus vivant, le plus jeune et le plus riche du XIXe siècle. C'est qu'il a su faire un large appel à l'imagination. C'est elle qui le guide dans ses évocations historiques, qui le conduit à donner comme toile de fond à *Lorenzaccio* une Italie de la Renaissance peinte des couleurs du rêve ou parfois du cauchemar. Chez lui, pas de souci faussement philosophique, mais simplement une vision du monde faite d'amertume et de nonchalance. Chez lui, pas d'exagération mélodramatique, mais une discrétion subtile, une résignation tout humaine. Il a réussi, par ailleurs, à marquer profondément de sa personnalité son œuvre théâtrale. Ses personnages ne sont pas des entités, mais des reflets de lui-même, des doubles qui lui ressemblent comme des frères et qui sont frémissants de sa sensibilité : Silvio de *A quoi rêvent les jeunes filles,* c'est le Musset enfant terrible, badin, sentimental, puéril ; Fantasio, c'est le Musset blessé, dissimulant sous l'excentricité sa tendresse humaine ; Lorenzaccio, c'est le Musset réprouvé, regrettant sa pureté évanouie...

Enfin, il a su, grâce à sa science du dialogue, donner à ses pièces une vie intense : connaissant à merveille la complexité des caractères humains, disposant avec habileté les plans, entourant les personnages principaux de figures stylisées (comme Dame Pluche, Blazius ou Bridaine de *On ne badine pas avec l'amour*), il aboutit à une grande efficacité de l'action et à une description vraie des êtres, saisis dans l'intimité de leur âme.

Théâtre éminemment humain que celui de Musset qui mérite bien sa place dans cet édifice du drame romantique tel que le rêvait Thibaudet : « Il en va donc du drame romantique comme de la cathédrale idéale qui devait avoir, dit-on, les clochers de Chartres, la façade de Reims, la nef d'Amiens, et le chœur de Beauvais. Ici, le vers de Hugo, la facture de Dumas, l'humanité de Musset, et la philosophie de Vigny[1]. »

1. Albert Thibaudet, *Histoire de la Littérature française de 1789 à nos jours*, Paris, Stock, 1946.

Histoire de l'œuvre $\boxed{3}$

LES SOURCES HISTORIQUES

Dans *Lorenzaccio*, Musset exploite des faits historiques précis, même si, on le constatera, il les modifie et les dénature quelque peu. L'action de la pièce se déroule à Florence en 1536-1537. Quelle est la situation politique de l'Italie au début de ce second tiers du XVIe siècle ?

Elle est d'une très grande complexité. Le pays n'est pas unifié, mais divisé, émietté en une multiplicité de cités et d'États indépendants. Trois puissances y exercent une influence déterminante : le pape, qui ne joue pas seulement un rôle spirituel, mais qui dispose alors d'une force politique et militaire redoutable ; Charles Quint, empereur germanique, qui possède d'immenses territoires en Europe et en Amérique ; le roi de France, François Ier, adversaire résolu de Charles Quint, qu'il affrontera, notamment en Italie, durant plus de trente ans.
La place de Florence dans ce dispositif est cruciale. D'abord républicaine, elle tombe progressivement sous la coupe de la puissante famille des Médicis. Chassés du pouvoir par les républicains en 1527, les Médicis font un retour triomphal en 1531. C'est qu'ils disposent de deux appuis efficaces : Charles Quint est leur allié et, depuis 1523, c'est un de leurs parents qui est pape sous le nom de Clément VII. Alexandre de Médicis devient duc de Florence et peut désormais exercer sans frein son autorité sur la ville, protégé par Charles Quint qui y installe une garnison. Dans ce contexte, François Ier soutient évidemment les républicains : il les a aidés au cours de leur révolte de 1527 ; il est toujours à leurs côtés après le retour des Médicis.

Et Lorenzaccio ? Fils de Pierre-François de Médicis et cousin d'Alexandre de Médicis, duc de Florence, il pouvait lui aussi prétendre au pouvoir et apparaît donc comme une des victimes de l'opération. Mais surtout, il est attiré par les idées républicaines. Dès lors, le rapport des forces est clair : d'un côté, Alexandre de Médicis soutenu par Charles Quint et, dans une moindre mesure, par le nouveau pape Paul III qui a succédé à Clément VII en 1534 ; de l'autre, les républicains appuyés par François Ier et jouant la carte de Lorenzaccio. Telle est la situation de départ dont découlent les événements : Lorenzaccio va s'efforcer de devenir le favori d'Alexandre de Médicis pour l'attirer dans un guet-apens et le tuer le 6 janvier 1537[1]. Les républicains ne parviendront pas à profiter des circonstances. Côme de Médicis, cousin d'Alexandre, réussira à perpétuer le régime un instant ébranlé. Lorenzaccio, contraint à l'exil, sera assassiné le 26 février 1548.

UNE CONVERGENCE D'INSPIRATIONS

Malgré leur importance dans le développement de l'action, les sources historiques ne peuvent rendre compte de toute la richesse de la conception. *Lorenzaccio* apparaît comme une œuvre composite, lieu de convergence d'inspirations multiples : l'élaboration par Musset de trois plans successifs de la pièce témoigne éloquemment de la difficulté qu'il éprouva à ordonner tous les éléments qu'il voulait y introduire.

Sous l'histoire florentine transparaissent tout d'abord des allusions évidentes à la situation contemporaine de Musset. Indirectement, il dénonce la veulerie et la lâcheté de ses compatriotes uniquement préoccupés de leur bien-être matériel, privés de tout idéal. Plus précisément, il regrette les occasions manquées : les républicains florentins laissant Côme de Médicis succéder à Alexandre, ce sont un peu les républicains français incapables de profiter de leur victoire et de la chute de

---

1. Musset situe le meurtre en 1536, certainement pour introduire le développement des « six six » du marchand (Acte V, scène 5), qui place cet événement sous le signe du chiffre six. Alexandre, après un règne de six ans, est mort en 1536, le six janvier, à six heures du matin, à l'âge de vingt-six ans, de six blessures.

Charles X en 1830, impuissants à empêcher le roi bourgeois Louis-Philippe de s'emparer du pouvoir.

Les sources littéraires sont nombreuses : au rôle prépondérant joué par *la Storia fiorentina,* chronique de Varchi du XVIe siècle qui ne fut publiée qu'au XVIIIe siècle, s'ajoute l'influence difficilement appréciable exercée par *une Conspiration en 1537,* sorte de canevas écrit par George Sand sur le même sujet que *Lorenzaccio.* Sous ces deux sources principales court tout un réseau souterrain. Shakespeare et le théâtre romantique allemand fournissent notamment à l'œuvre son atmosphère sombre et son sens des grands mouvements de foule. Et le personnage de Lorenzaccio doit beaucoup au personnage shakespearien, Hamlet : il lui a donné son aspiration à l'absolu, sa persévérance à traquer le mal, sa conviction désespérée selon laquelle il n'est pas possible d'agir sans se salir les mains, cette idée que la pureté perdue ne peut jamais se retrouver.

Enfin, bien sûr, *Lorenzaccio* est empli de la sensibilité de Musset, de cette sensibilité à fleur de peau qui commence à le marquer dans ces années 1830.

1833-1834 : UNE GESTATION DOULOUREUSE

Lorsque, en 1833, Musset entreprend la rédaction de *Lorenzaccio*, qui passe, à juste titre, pour être son chef-d'œuvre théâtral, il a vingt-trois ans. Il est donc en pleine jeunesse, mais déjà à la moitié de sa brève existence qui s'achèvera vingt-quatre ans plus tard. Une époque de sa vie vient de se terminer, celle de l'enfance studieuse et de l'adolescence agitée et insouciante, la période de formation et de dandysme, le temps de la production brillante, mais un peu superficielle qui le fait considérer comme « l'enfant terrible » du romantisme.

George Sand va se charger de lui faire connaître à satiété l'agitation, les désillusions, les retournements de la passion. C'est durant l'été 1833 qu'il fera sa connaissance ; c'est en décembre qu'ils partent tous deux en Italie où se nouera le drame. Après avoir parcouru le pays et s'être notamment arrêtés à Florence, ils arrivent à Venise. En janvier 1834, le poète y tombe gravement malade et voit s'ajouter à la souffrance physique la torture morale d'assister à la liaison de George Sand avec son propre médecin, le docteur Pagello. Ce sont des scènes interminables et sans cesse renouvelées ; et finalement, le 29 mars, Musset , vaincu, quitte Venise et rentre à Paris. C'est dans ce contexte tour à tour passionné et douloureux que seront écrites trois de ses œuvres majeures : *Fantasio, On ne badine pas avec l'amour* et *Lorenzaccio*, à l'atmosphère sombre entrecoupée de quelques échappées de lumière...

Une lettre envoyée par Musset le 27 janvier 1834 à Buloz, le directeur de la *Revue des deux mondes*, prouve que *Lorenzaccio* est achevé avant le départ pour l'Italie et la rupture avec George Sand : aussi l'œuvre présente-t-elle, par endroits, une vision du monde qui n'est pas totalement obscurcie par le désespoir. La pièce sera publiée en août 1834 dans la nouvelle édition en deux volumes d'*Un spectacle dans un fauteuil*.

Après l'échec de la création de *la Nuit vénitienne* en 1830, Musset s'était juré de ne plus faire représenter ses pièces. L'élaboration même de *Lorenzaccio*, conçu pour être lu et non pour être joué, aurait créé d'ailleurs des difficultés de mise en scène. Et les allusions politiques indirectes à la France de 1830 constituaient un obstacle supplémentaire. Aucune représentation n'eut donc lieu du vivant de Musset. La première ne fut donnée qu'en 1896, avec Sarah Bernhardt dans le rôle de Lorenzaccio (voir p.74).

Les moments de l'action : analyse de la pièce

4

Cinq actes, trente-huit scènes, quarante personnages précisément dénommés, des dizaines de figurants, vingt décors différents, oui, vraiment, *Lorenzaccio* est une lourde machine dont il est bien difficile de démonter les rouages, tant ils sont nombreux, tant leur agencement est complexe. Enlèvements, duels, empoisonnements et complots, fausse vertu et débauche feinte, désœuvrement efficace et vaine agitation, tourments intérieurs et mouvements de foule, complexité individuelle et symbolisme collectif, assurément, *Lorenzaccio* se présente comme un édifice somptueux dont la décoration extérieure masque les grands choix architecturaux. Une analyse minutieuse est donc indispensable, si l'on veut saisir les orientations essentielles de l'œuvre, si l'on veut comprendre les intentions profondes de son auteur.

UNE DISTRIBUTION COMPLEXE

Les personnages sont nombreux, les liens qui les unissent ou les oppositions qui les séparent ne sont pas toujours d'une grande clarté. Une rapide étude de la distribution aidera à mieux se rendre compte d'une situation marquée par la complexité.

La famille Médicis

Alexandre de Médicis, duc de Florence, fils de Laurent II de Médicis. Côme de Médicis, son cousin, qui sera proclamé duc à sa mort.	soutenus par l'empereur d'Allemagne
Lorenzo de Médicis, cousin d'Alexandre. Marie Soderini, sa mère. Catherine Ginori, sa tante.	partisans des républicains

Les républicains

Philippe Strozzi, maître à penser. Pierre Strozzi. Léon Strozzi, prieur de Capoue. Thomas Strozzi.	ses fils
Louise Strozzi.	sa fille
Le petit Strozzi.	son petit-fils
Le provéditeur gouverneur de la citadelle Roberto Corsini	
Palla Ruccellaï, membre du Conseil des Huit. Alamanno Salviati. François Pazzi.	seigneurs républicains
Bindo Altoviti, oncle de Lorenzo. Venturi, bourgeois.	

La famille Cibo

La marquise Cibo, républicaine de cœur, maîtresse du duc.
Le marquis Cibo, son mari.
Ascanio, leur jeune fils.
Le cardinal Cibo, frère du marquis, à la puissance occulte redoutable.

L'entourage

Sire Maurice, chancelier de l'assemblée judiciaire, le Conseil des Huit.

Niccolini.
Vettori.
Capponi.
Acciaiuoli.
Canigiani.
Corsi.

membres du Conseil des Huit, hostiles à la République.

Julien Salviati, un des favoris du duc.
Le petit Salviati, son fils.
Giomo, âme damnée du duc.
Scoronconcolo, homme de confiance de Lorenzaccio.

Jean.
Pippo.

hommes de confiance de Philippe Strozzi.

Le cardinal Baccio Valori, commissaire apostolique, envoyé du pape.
Guicciardini, historien.

Personnages divers

Maffio, un bourgeois.
Gabrielle, sa sœur.
Tebaldeo, peintre.
Agnolo, page.

Un orfèvre, un marchand, un officier allemand, un portier, un médecin, un masque, deux dames de la cour, deux cavaliers, deux écoliers, deux gentilshommes, deux précepteurs, les membres de la famille Strozzi, des femmes, des pages, des serviteurs, des courtisans, des moines, des novices, des gens du peuple, des soldats, des gardes, des bannis.

ACTE I
FLORENCE : LES FORCES EN PRÉSENCE

Dans ce premier acte, Musset poursuit un double but : procéder à un vaste panorama historique des mœurs florentines ; situer les personnages sur l'échiquier politique, tout en laissant planer l'ambiguïté sur Lorenzaccio.

SCÈNE 1 : [Un exemple des mœurs corrompues de la cour ducale, l'enlèvement de Gabrielle].

Après une longue attente par un clair de lune romantique, le duc de Médicis, son écuyer et Lorenzaccio enlèvent une jeune fille qu'ils ont débauchée à prix d'or. Son frère, Maffio, qui essayait de s'opposer au rapt par la force, est désarmé.

SCÈNE 2 : [Le faste de quelques-uns est-il le symbole de la grandeur et du bonheur de Florence ?].

Scène de foule et conversations séparées : les écoliers ne voient que le côté pittoresque et amusant de cette richesse étalée ; le marchand se réjouit, car les fêtes font marcher le commerce ; l'orfèvre s'élève contre l'oisiveté des grands qui ne paient pas toujours leurs dettes, et contre l'occupation allemande qui pèse sur la cité ; enfin, élément important pour le déroulement de l'action, Julien Salviati, favori du duc, poursuit de ses grossières assiduités Louise, de la famille républicaine des Strozzi.

SCÈNE 3 : [Les dangers de la sensibilité].

C'est ici qu'intervient le début de l'intrigue qui va lier, un moment, la marquise Cibo et le duc. Le cardinal Cibo, qui a intercepté la correspondance de sa belle-sœur, est au courant de cet amour naissant. Voilà qui permet à Musset de souligner les contradictions de la femme et d'insister sur les dangers de la sensibilité. La construction, tout en antithèses, oppose aux couleurs pastel de la scène d'intérieur baignée de larmes et de tendres réminiscences entre le marquis, sa femme et leur fils, le machiavélisme du cardinal et ses propos cyniques sur la réalité qu'il vient de découvrir.

SCÈNE 4 : [Lorenzetta ou Lorenzo de Médicis ?].

De la maison des Cibo, nous voici transportés auprès du duc de Médicis. Le duc prend la défense de Lorenzo qui a été mis en cause par Sire Maurice et par le cardinal Cibo. Le pape, disent-ils, reproche à Lorenzo d'être un débauché ? Qu'il pense donc à son propre fils, Pierre Farnèse. Ils insinuent qu'il n'est pas politiquement sûr ? Que chacun sache qu'il sert d'indicateur et qu'il fournit de nombreux renseignements sur les républicains. Lorenzaccio, survenu sur ces entrefaites et provoqué en duel par Sire Maurice qu'il a outragé, confirme le duc dans son opinion ; il s'évanouit à la vue de l'épée, ce qui lui vaut ces railleries : « Allons ! chère Lorenzetta, fais-toi emporter chez ta mère ».

SCÈNE 5 : [La provocation].

Cette scène est le pendant de la scène 2 : la première partie, consacrée à ces grands mouvements de foule qu'affectionne Musset, brosse le tableau de Florence divisée, comme le montrent les conversations des pèlerins devant l'église de Saint-Miniato, entre les soutiens du pouvoir et les républicains. La seconde partie concerne directement l'action. Il s'agit d'une véritable provocation : Salviati, un des favoris du duc, affirme au prieur, un des fils du républicain Strozzi, que sa sœur Louise lui a promis de lui accorder ses faveurs.

SCÈNE 6 : [Lorenzo et les républicains].

Là encore, Musset lie situation individuelle et situation collective : d'une part, il met en scène une conversation entre la mère de Lorenzo, Marie Soderini et sa tante, Catherine, qui déplorent sa lâcheté et sa conduite ambiguë envers les républicains ; parallèlement, il brosse une description d'ensemble, et présente en train de quitter Florence ceux qui ont peut-être été bannis sur dénonciation de Lorenzo.

ACTE II
LA CONFUSION DES OPINIONS ET DES SENTIMENTS

Dans cet acte, éclate toute l'ambiguïté des rapports entre le pouvoir en place et ses adversaires, tandis que sont posées les contradictions qui existent souvent entre la pensée et l'action.

SCÈNE I : [S'indigner ou agir ?].

Dans cette scène, pour la première fois dans *Lorenzaccio,* Musset se penche sur les contradictions qui caractérisent souvent l'activité politique. Nous sommes chez les républicains Strozzi. Le père, Philippe, exprime son désarroi dans un monologue : comme beaucoup de penseurs, il appréhende difficilement le concret.

Deux de ses fils, le prieur et Pierre, faisant leur entrée, une conversation s'engage sur la provocation dont a été victime Louise, ce qui permet de dégager trois attitudes différentes devant l'action : le prieur, c'est l'oubli raisonnable (« Allons, voilà qui est fait, je n'y penserai pas davantage ») ; Philippe Strozzi, c'est la prudence réfléchie (« Allons, dit-il à Pierre, es-tu fait de salpêtre[1] ? Qu'as-tu à faire de cette épée ? ») ; Pierre Strozzi, c'est l'activisme irresponsable (« c'est-à-dire, que cela me démange de lui couper les oreilles »).

SCÈNE 2 : [L'art est un engagement total].

Cette scène peut paraître extérieure à l'action. Mais si Musset ouvre une parenthèse pour exprimer sa conception de l'art, il n'en oublie pas pour autant les nécessités de l'intrigue, et se sert de cet exposé pour mieux dégager la personnalité de Lorenzaccio. Le décor représente le portail d'une église. Une

---

1. « Es-tu fait de salpêtre ? » : es-tu prêt à t'enflammer au premier instant ? Le salpêtre était l'un des trois composants de la poudre à canon.

conversation s'engage entre Lorenzaccio, Valori (commissaire apostolique) et le peintre Tebaldeo Freccia. Valori insiste sur la signification esthétique de la religion (« L'artiste ne trouverait-t-il pas là le paradis de son cœur ? ») ; Tebaldeo considère l'art comme une activité complète qui fait appel à la fois à la piété, à l'imagination, au patriotisme, à la souffrance et à la liberté ; Lorenzaccio, après avoir exprimé son nihilisme, invite le peintre à venir, le lendemain, au palais du duc, « faire un tableau d'importance ».

SCÈNE 3 : [Religion et ambition, politique et sentiments].

L'action se déroule, à nouveau, chez la marquise Cibo. Le cardinal est bien décidé à profiter de ses fonctions de confesseur pour connaître l'évolution de l'intrigue amoureuse qui lie sa belle-sœur au duc de Médicis : dévoué à l'empereur Charles Quint et au pape, il pense exploiter la situation dans des buts politiques, faire pression sur Alexandre de Médicis pour l'amener à renforcer ses liens avec eux. La marquise, après avoir reconnu en confession qu'elle a donné un rendez-vous au duc, se demande si l'action qu'elle mène est inspirée par l'amour ou par son attachement à Florence (« Et pourquoi est-ce que tu te mêles à tout cela, toi, Florence ? Qui est-ce donc que j'aime ? Est-ce toi ? Est-ce lui ? »).

SCÈNE 4 : [Lorenzaccio est-il un traître ?].

L'ambiguïté de l'attitude de Lorenzaccio est portée ici à son comble. Au début de la scène, il s'entretient avec Catherine et Marie, sa mère et sa tante, et achève cette conversation en annonçant un événement qui « étonnera ». Arrivent deux républicains, Bindo et Venturi, qui le prient avec insistance de préciser ses positions. Cette discussion est bientôt interrompue par l'intrusion inattendue d'Alexandre de Médicis qui accorde aux deux hommes les faveurs malicieusement sollicitées pour eux par Lorenzaccio : l'expérience est concluante, ils acceptent, malgré les protestations de principe prononcées, précaution oblige, à voix basse. La scène s'achève sur la demande du duc à Lorenzaccio de lui présenter sa tante dont il a admiré la beauté. Et Lorenzaccio part pour la maison des Strozzi, en apportant ces précisions pleines de sous-entendus : « Si vous saviez comme cela est aisé de mentir impudemment au nez d'un butor [1] ».

SCÈNE 5 : [L'attente et la vengeance].

L'atmosphère est dramatique dans le palais de la famille républicaine des Strozzi. Philippe Strozzi, son fils, le prieur et sa fille Louise, attendent, dans l'angoisse, en compagnie de Lorenzaccio, le retour de Pierre Strozzi qu'ils savent décidé à venger l'affront fait à Louise par Julien Salviati, favori du duc. L'arrivée de Pierre justifie ces appréhensions : il vient, dit-il, de tuer Salviati.

SCÈNE 6 : [Le peintre et la cotte de mailles].

Au palais ducal. Un mélange bien dosé de raffinement et de sauvagerie, de luxe et de cruauté : Giomo, protégé du duc, chante une chanson tendre, et vient de tuer un jeune garçon du voisinage ; le duc se fait faire son portrait par Tebaldeo, et parle de sa cotte de mailles. Un pas important pour la progression de l'action : Lorenzo subtilise la cotte de mailles du duc et lui annonce que sa tante, Catherine, accepte le rendez-vous qu'il a sollicité de sa part.

SCÈNE 7 : [Salviati rescapé].

Salviati, gravement blessé, vient réclamer justice au duc qui termine l'acte sur ces paroles pleines de menaces : « Par Hercule ! les meurtriers passeront la nuit en prison, et on les pendra demain matin ».

---

1. *Butor* : personne grossière, sans délicatesse.

ACTE III
LA PRÉPARATION DU MEURTRE

C'est le tournant de l'action : alors que les différentes tentatives des républicains sont brisées, Lorenzaccio révèle sa véritable personnalité et met au point son plan.

SCÈNE 1 : [Un drôle de jeu].

Dans sa chambre à coucher, Lorenzo se livre avec le spadassin[1] Scoronconcolo à un jeu étrange : cris, appels au secours, le vacarme est épouvantable. Le but ? Lorenzo le laisse facilement deviner : habituer les voisins à ces scènes de meurtre. La raison ? il l'indique clairement à Scoronconcolo : « Tu as deviné mon mal, j'ai un ennemi. Mais pour lui je ne me servirai pas d'une épée qui ait servi pour d'autres. Celle qui le tuera n'aura ici-bas qu'un baptême ; elle gardera son nom ». C'est un assassinat qui se prépare.

SCÈNE 2 : [Quand il n'est plus temps pour la pensée].

Le père, Philippe, et le fils, Pierre, s'affrontent au palais des Strozzi, l'un préférant l'action réfléchie et l'autre l'action immédiate. Le père se laisse finalement convaincre : « Depuis quand le vieil aigle reste-t-il dans le nid, quand ses aiglons vont à la curée ? » et accompagne son fils chez les Pazzi où a lieu une réunion des républicains.

SCÈNE 3 : [Le vrai Lorenzo].

Il s'agit là de la partie centrale de la pièce, par la position qu'elle occupe au début de l'Acte III, par sa longueur qui en fait un véritable morceau de bravoure et surtout par les réflexions sur l'action et la pureté qu'elle développe. La scène se déroule

---

1. *Spadassin :* homme d'épée, homme de main, assassin à gages.

dans la rue et débute par l'arrestation de Pierre et Thomas Strozzi, malgré les protestations de leur père, Philippe, et des passants. Après un monologue dans lequel il désespère de son bon droit, Philippe Strozzi engage un long dialogue avec Lorenzaccio. Ce dernier explique le danger de l'idéal et l'inanité d'une action dont les résultats seront de toute manière trahis par ceux à qui elle devrait profiter. Il se montre alors sous son véritable visage : celui d'un jeune homme qui a tout sacrifié à ses aspirations et surtout sa pureté, salie irrémédiablement, qui « glisse depuis deux ans sur un rocher taillé a pic », si bien que le meurtre du duc est « le seul brin d'herbe » auquel il puisse se raccrocher.

SCÈNE 4 : [Une lettre du duc pour Catherine].

Au palais Soderini, Catherine, tante de Lorenzo, lit à Marie une lettre du duc demandant un rendez-vous. Il apparaît que Lorenzaccio a joué auprès de sa tante le rôle d'entremetteur, ce qui plonge sa mère dans le désespoir.

SCÈNE 5 : [La marquise se prépare à recevoir le duc].

La marquise Cibo un instant interrompue par le cardinal, qui rôde comme un « vautour à tête chauve », se prépare à recevoir le duc, partagée entre la curiosité et l'angoisse.

SCÈNE 6 : [L'échec politique de la séduction].

Dans son boudoir, la marquise Cibo essaie de persuader le duc de changer ses principes de gouvernement, en faisant triompher la liberté et en travaillant au bonheur du peuple. Mais Alexandre de Médicis ne se laisse pas convaincre : ce qui le préoccupe, c'est de tirer le plus d'argent possible de ses sujets. Ce qu'il demande à la marquise, c'est de se contenter d'utiliser la séduction de son corps, c'est de jouer son « petit rôle de femme, et de vraie femme ». C'est donc l'échec politique sanctionné par le départ du duc dont le cardinal est témoin. C'est aussi la tragédie personnelle de la marquise qui, un peu tard, exprime son désespoir, à la pensée d'avoir « voué au ridicule » son mari Laurent.

SCÈNE 7 : [L'empoisonnement de Louise Strozzi].

Chez les Strozzi, c'est un véritable conseil de guerre. Philippe, mis hors de lui par l'arrestation de ses fils, est enfin décidé à passer à l'action. Les convives boivent « A la mort des Médicis », lorsqu'éclate le drame : Louise tombe morte, empoisonnée. Le coup est trop rude pour Philippe qui, à demi fou, abandonne toutes ses résolutions, et ne trouve qu'à répéter : « Dieu de justice ! Dieu de justice ! que t'ai-je fait ? »

ACTE IV
L'EXÉCUTION DU MEURTRE

Face à l'impuissance des républicains, Lorenzaccio passe enfin à l'action : il attire le duc dans un guet-apens et l'assassine.

SCÈNE 1 : [Le piège se referme].

Le fauve : le duc ; le chasseur : Lorenzaccio ; l'aide : Scoronconcolo ; l'appât : Catherine ; les précautions : le vol de la cotte de mailles ; le lieu : la chambre de Lorenzaccio. Tout est prêt. Il n'est plus que la nuit à attendre.

SCÈNE 2 : [La fureur de Pierre].

Les deux frères de Louise Strozzi, libérés, apprennent la mort de leur sœur. Pierre clame sa fureur et ses désirs de vengeance : « Venez, venez, avant que je perde la force. Ne me dites pas un mot ; il s'agit là d'une vengeance, voyez-vous ! telle que la colère céleste n'en a pas rêvé ».

SCÈNE 3 : [Lorenzaccio, « le bras de Dieu » ?].

Après avoir donné rendez-vous à Scoronconcolo pour minuit, Lorenzaccio s'interroge sur son rôle : « Suis-je le bras de Dieu ? Y a-t-il une nuée au-dessus de ma tête ? Quand j'entrerai dans cette chambre, et que je voudrai tirer mon épée du fourreau, j'ai peur de tirer l'épée flamboyante de l'archange et de tomber en cendres sur ma proie ».

SCÈNE 4 : [La marquise renonce au duc].

Le cardinal Cibo révèle tout son machiavélisme. Après avoir averti la marquise qu'il est au courant de ses relations avec Alexandre, il lui met le marché en main : ou bien, elle fait tous ses efforts pour demeurer la maîtresse en titre du duc et il se sert d'elle pour réaliser ses desseins politiques ; ou bien, elle refuse et il la dénonce à son mari. Mais c'est la marquise, repoussant enfin la compromission, qui avouera tout à son époux : « Laurent, pendant que vous étiez à Massa, je me suis livrée à Alexandre (...), sachant qui il était, et quel rôle misérable j'allais jouer ».

SCÈNE 5 : [La souillure est indélébile].

Lorenzo, dans sa chambre, met la dernière main aux préparatifs du meurtre, lorsqu'arrive Catherine. Elle lui parle des propositions du duc. Il exprime alors, presque malgré lui, des doutes sur la pureté de sa tante et constate, après son départ, que la débauche est installée en lui, que la souillure est indélébile : « Le vice, comme la robe de Déjanire [1], s'est-il si profondément incorporé à mes fibres, que je ne puisse plus répondre de ma langue, et que l'air qui sort de mes lèvres se fasse ruffian malgré moi ? »

SCÈNE 6 : [La fin justifie-t-elle les moyens ?].

C'est à nouveau le problème de l'action qui est posé dans cette scène. Après l'enterrement de Louise, Pierre Strozzi apporte à son père Philippe une lettre de François 1er qui lui propose son secours. Tandis que le père refuse ce qu'il considère comme une trahison, le fils ne craint pas de se salir les mains. C'est la rupture.

SCÈNE 7 : [Lorenzo essaie (en vain) de mobiliser les républicains].

Lorenzaccio frappe aux portes des palais du bord de l'Arno, fleuve qui baigne Florence, pour annoncer l'assassinat pro-

---

1. Déjanire causa la mort de son mari Héraclès, en lui faisant revêtir une tunique empoisonnée qui s'incrusta dans son corps.

chain du duc et amener ainsi les républicains à agir. Il n'est pas pris au sérieux et ne peut que se lamenter : « Pauvre Florence ! pauvre Florence !».

SCÈNE 8 : [Pierre ne recule devant rien].

Pierre Strozzi, n'arrivant pas à convaincre les bannis d'agir sans Philippe, s'en va sur ces menaces adressées à l'envoyé : « Va au diable, canaille ! et dis à tes confédérés que, s'ils ne veulent pas de moi, le roi de France en veut, lui ! et qu'ils prennent garde qu'on ne me donne la main haute sur vous tous ! »

SCÈNE 9 : [Lorenzo dans l'attente du meurtre].

C'est la nuit ; sur une place, Lorenzaccio attend, avec impatience et angoisse, le moment du meurtre. Dans un long monologue, passant sans cesse d'un sujet à l'autre, à la recherche de son équilibre, il procède à une véritable répétition de la scène tragique qui va se dérouler, tout en se remémorant les souvenirs de sa jeunesse paisible.

SCÈNE 10 : [« La volonté de Dieu se fait malgré les hommes »].

Au palais ducal, le bruit des démarches entreprises par Lorenzaccio se répand. Le duc attribue l'attitude du jeune homme à l'ivresse et n'hésite pas à partir avec lui, lorsqu'il vient le chercher à minuit pour le rendez-vous avec Catherine.

SCÈNE 11 : [L'assassinat libérateur].

Le duc, arrivé chez Lorenzo, se couche. Et c'est l'assassinat, qui inquiète Scoronconcolo, lorsqu'il s'aperçoit de l'identité du mort, mais qui libère l'assassin en lui faisant retrouver une certaine pureté : « Que le vent du soir est doux et embaumé ! comme les fleurs des prairies s'entrouvrent ! ô nature magnifique ! ô éternel repos ! ».

ACTE V
L'ÉCHEC

Les républicains sont impuissants à exploiter l'assassinat du duc. La tyrannie se maintient à Florence : c'est l'échec de l'action de Lorenzaccio qui cherche la mort et la trouve.

SCÈNE 1 : [La succession d'Alexandre de Médicis].

Grand remue-ménage au palais ducal le lendemain matin. Le duc a disparu : le bruit de sa mort se répand. On décide de taire la nouvelle, afin de prendre toutes dispositions utiles : les visiteurs sont renvoyés ; le peuple est apaisé par des distributions de vivres. Les discussions sur la succession vont leur train : les propositions les plus saugrenues sont avancées. Le cardinal Cibo, qui a visiblement la situation en main, fait finalement élire Côme de Médicis, cousin du duc assassiné. Vettori tire la leçon des événements et de l'apparente improvisation si bien orchestrée par le cardinal : « Que voulez-vous ? notre vote est fait, et il est probable qu'il acceptera. Tout cela est étourdissant ».

SCÈNE 2 : [La tête de Lorenzaccio est mise à prix].

A Venise, Philippe Strozzi déplore que Pierre ait accepté l'offre de s'allier avec François 1er. Lorenzo lui apprend la mort du duc, mais lui prédit l'inaction des républicains : la proclamation qui met sa tête à prix confirme ses craintes.

SCÈNE 3 : [Le marquis Cibo a pardonné].

Il se promène dans une rue de Florence avec sa femme, ce qui provoque les commentaires de deux gentilshommes.

SCÈNE 4 : [L'ambition de Pierre Strozzi].

Il est bien décidé à profiter des circonstances : « Quoi qu'il en soit, une route s'ouvre devant moi, sur laquelle il y a plus de bons grains que de poussière ».

SCÈNE 5 : [Le résultat de l'action de Lorenzaccio : des mots, des mots, des mots].

Dans les rues de Florence, l'effervescence s'apaise. Tout n'est plus que mots : le marchand fait remarquer à l'orfèvre que la mort du duc est placée sous le signe du chiffre six ; l'orfèvre déplore que l'occasion n'ait pas été saisie par les républicains ; le petit Strozzi et le petit Salviati se disputent, continuant la querelle qui oppose leurs deux familles, tandis que leurs précepteurs dissertent.

SCÈNE 6 : [Une seule issue pour Lorenzaccio : la mort].

La scène est à nouveau chez Philippe Strozzi, à Venise. Lorenzo vient d'apprendre la mort de sa mère. Après des paroles désabusées sur lui-même et sur ses semblables, malgré les conseils de prudence de Philippe, il sort, se fait tuer par la foule et jeter dans la lagune.

SCÈNE 7 : [Le duc est mort, vive le duc !].

Sur la grande place de Florence, Côme de Médicis, couronné duc par le cardinal, prononce le discours d'usage...

L'organisation de la pièce : action, lieu, temps

A lire le résumé de la pièce, *Lorenzaccio* frappe par sa complexité. Les intrigues s'enchevêtrent sans ordre apparent. Les lieux se succèdent. Le temps s'écoule. Mais, paradoxalement, ce texte, conçu, à l'origine, pour la lecture, ne prend sa véritable dimension, sa véritable logique qu'à la représentation : grâce au schématisme que créent les conditions du spectacle, les grandes masses s'ordonnent ; l'ensemble trouve son équilibre, et son unité apparaît dans toute sa signification et dans toute sa cohérence.

LA CONDUITE DE L'ACTION

Le sens de la pièce est clair : sur un fond historique qui plonge le spectateur dans l'Italie du XVIe siècle, s'inscrivent les tentatives pour transformer le système politique en place, pour en finir avec le régime autoritaire qui s'est installé. A ce niveau historique, s'ajoute un niveau philosophique qui amène à poser, sur le plan individuel et collectif, les problèmes de l'action et de la pureté.

C'est dans ce cadre que se développent les intrigues, que l'on appelle encore les fils de la pièce. Elles sont au nombre de cinq : Lorenzaccio (intrigue 1), les républicains, qui se divisent, par la suite, en deux camps, celui de Philippe Strozzi (intrigue 2) et celui de son fils Pierre (intrigue 3), la marquise Cibo (intrigue 4) et la masse anonyme des habitants de Florence (intrigue 5) affrontent, avec des moyens et des objectifs divers, le tyran Alexandre de Médicis.

Faut-il en conclure à une absence d'unité d'action ? Oui, en apparence, d'autant plus que ces cinq intrigues se déroulent de façon relativement autonome. Non, en fait, car des liens viennent les relier : c'est la faillite de l'opposition républicaine organisée qui amène Lorenzaccio et la marquise d'abord, Pierre ensuite, à chercher des formes d'action moins classiques ; c'est l'abandon de la marquise par le duc qui permet à Lorenzaccio d'attirer sa victime dans un piège ; c'est pour les républicains et pour le peuple que Lorenzaccio travaille. Et puis, surtout, il s'agit de cinq tentatives dirigées contre le pouvoir représenté par un obstacle apparent, le duc, et par un obstacle occulte, le cardinal. Il s'agit de cinq formes d'action qui toutes échouent. Chacun de ces cinq fils est conduit avec son exposition, son développement et son dénouement.

Première intrigue : Lorenzaccio et l'engagement total

L'intrigue essentielle est évidemment celle qui concerne Lorenzaccio : c'est lui qui donne son nom à la pièce et il y occupe 17 scènes sur 38. C'est l'histoire de l'engagement total d'un être dans l'action. Pour parvenir à ses fins, pour éliminer le tyran, il ne recule devant rien, il a tout misé, tout sacrifié, jusqu'à sa pureté, et constate avec désespoir qu'il s'est sali les mains, que, dans un souci d'efficacité, il est allé jusqu'à la destruction de ses valeurs les plus chères.

L'exposition, qui consiste à fournir les données nécessaires à la compréhension de la situation, est fort longue. Elle se prolonge jusqu'au début de l'Acte III. Musset entretient savamment le suspense, en maintenant le plus longtemps possible les doutes sur la véritable personnalité de Lorenzaccio. Est-il un débauché, définitivement perverti ? Est-il, au contraire, un être désintéressé qui travaille pour le bonheur de Florence ? Cette ambiguïté ne se dissipe qu'à la scène I de l'Acte III. Le but que poursuit Lorenzaccio se révèle enfin, lorsqu'il confie à Scoronconcolo : « Tu as deviné mon mal, j'ai un ennemi » et désigne ainsi sa cible, Alexandre de Médicis.

La technique adoptée présente deux particularités qui la distinguent des procédés de l'exposition traditionnelle et créent le dynamisme : Musset utilise l'effet de surprise qui repose sur le jeu des apparences et de la réalité et enchâsse habilement, à l'intérieur de l'exposé des faits, deux données, le vol de la cotte de mailles (Acte II, scène 6) et la lutte avec Scoronconcolo (Acte III, scène 1), qui font déjà partie de la conduite de l'intrigue.

Une fois qu'a été indiqué au spectateur tout ce qui est nécessaire à la compréhension des faits, Lorenzaccio va se trouver partagé entre la préparation de son plan (Acte IV, scènes 1, 3, 5, 9), les efforts de dissimulation de son projet au duc (Acte IV, scènes 1 et 10) et les avertissements donnés aux républicains (Acte III, scène 3 ; Acte IV, scène 7).

Pour animer l'action, trois coups de théâtre interviennent, mais ils ne provoquent pas de rebondissements spectaculaires : à la scène 7 de l'Acte IV, le refus des républicains de prendre Lorenzaccio au sérieux n'aura pas d'influence sur l'action entreprise, mais pèsera lourd sur ses conséquences. A la scène 1 de l'Acte IV, la méfiance du duc au constat du vol de sa cotte de mailles, enfin, à la scène 10 de l'Acte IV, les avertissements du cardinal Cibo auraient pu compromettre le déroulement du plan. Mais il n'en est rien : ces épisodes ne connaissent pas en effet de véritable développement.

L'action ne comporte donc que peu de rebondissements et rend parfaitement compte de la logique implacable avec laquelle Lorenzaccio conduit ses desseins. Trois scènes seulement sont consacrées au dénouement qui se déroule pourtant en deux temps : à la scène 11 de l'Acte IV, c'est la disparition de l'obstacle avec l'assassinat du duc ; à la scène 6 de l'Acte V, c'est la mort de Lorenzo, dont la tête a été mise à prix (Acte V, scène 2).

C'est là une fin significative qui montre que le véritable obstacle, ce n'était pas le duc. Il ne l'était pas politiquement, puisqu'il est aussitôt remplacé. Il ne l'était pas personnellement pour Lorenzaccio, dont le mal est, à l'évidence, tapi au fond même de l'âme.

Deuxième et troisième intrigues : Philippe et Pierre Strozzi, la pensée ou l'action

L'action menée par Philippe et Pierre Strozzi occupe 15 scènes sur les 38 que compte la pièce. Les deux intrigues se développent avec une symétrie parfaite. Elles représentent les deux réponses données par les républicains au pouvoir dictatorial : la patience et le compromis préconisés par le père, Philippe (11 scènes) ; la violence et l'irresponsabilité adoptées par le fils, Pierre (12 scènes).

L'exposition est commune aux deux actions. Elle ne s'étend pas au-delà du premier acte. Elle est dynamique. Elle montre concrètement la situation politique, la lutte sourde qui oppose le régime du duc aux républicains, en mettant en scène des affrontements individuels, comme l'insulte faite à Louise Strozzi par Salviati, et la persécution collective symbolisée par le bannissement des opposants.

C'est cet ensemble de données qui entraîne les réactions de Philippe et de Pierre Strozzi. La conduite du père, homme de pensée, philosophe, est marquée par l'indécision, les revirements, mais aussi le désintéressement. Le comportement du fils, homme d'action, est, au contraire, placé sous le signe de la détermination, mais aussi de l'ambition. Partis d'une analyse identique, ils vont donc suivre des chemins totalement différents.

Contrairement à ce qui se passe pour Lorenzaccio, cette double intrigue est marquée par des coups de théâtre importants : ils soulignent les contradictions entre la conduite du père et celle du fils et influent, de façon différente et même opposée, sur les desseins des deux hommes. L'échec de l'assassinat de Salviati (Acte II, scène 7), l'arrestation de Pierre et de Thomas (Acte III, scène 3), la mort de Louise (Acte III, scène 7), autant de faits qui plongent Philippe dans le désespoir et la résignation, Pierre dans la fureur et le désir de vengeance.

Le dénouement se produit en deux temps. Les deux hommes, dont les conceptions apparaissent irrémédiablement inconciliables, se séparent (Acte IV, scène 6) : Philippe se retire à Venise, renonce à l'action et consacre sa vie à des études stériles (Acte V, scènes 2 et 6), tandis que Pierre, dévoré d'ambition, devient un activiste prêt à tout pour faire triompher sa cause (Acte IV, scène 8 ; Acte V, scène 4). Mais, pour l'un et l'autre, l'élection de Côme de Médicis sonne comme un échec.

Quatrième intrigue : la marquise, ou la voie de la sensibilité

C'est toute sa sensibilité qu'engage la marquise Cibo pour faire pression sur les événements : éprise d'Alexandre de Médicis, elle espère l'amener par la force de son amour à modifier sa politique et à faire triompher la liberté.

Cette intrigue, somme toute accessoire, ne se déroule que sur 6 scènes : une rapide exposition (Acte I, scène 3) révèle en action les liens qui existent entre le duc et la marquise. Un développement en trois scènes raconte l'histoire d'un bref amour traversé par quelques cas de conscience : c'est, à la scène 3 de l'Acte II, la confession de la marquise au cardinal, son beau-frère ; à la scène 5 de l'Acte III, l'attente angoissée de l'arrivée du duc ; à la scène 6 de l'Acte III, l'impossible amour entre deux êtres qui ne peuvent se comprendre.

Le dénouement intervient en deux temps, avec l'aveu de la marquise à son mari (Acte IV, scène 4) et la réconciliation finale des deux époux (Acte V, scène 3). La mort du duc et l'élection de Côme de Médicis ne sont, à aucun moment, commentées par la marquise : voilà qui souligne que cette aventure politico-amoureuse n'est qu'un épisode accidentel dans sa vie.

Cinquième intrigue : l'impuissance du peuple de Florence

La dernière intrigue est une intrigue collective qui met en scène le peuple de Florence et son impuissance à agir : dans ce cadre, 9 scènes présentent la situation politique globale. L'exposition dépeint le mécontentement général (Acte I, scène 2). Puis l'action se développe ; tour à tour, prennent place sur le théâtre la contestation (Acte I, scène 5), le bannissement des partisans de la liberté (Acte I, scène 6), les protestations de la foule (Acte III, scène 3), le refus des républicains d'écouter les avertissements de Lorenzo qui constitue un semblant de coup de théâtre (Acte IV, scène 7), l'absence de réaction des opposants qui permet aux partisans du pouvoir en place de s'organiser (Acte V, scène 1), les bavardages stériles (Acte V, scène 5).

Toutes ces attitudes laissent présager le dénouement : l'avènement de Côme de Médicis (Acte V, scène 7), qui suit l'assassinat de Lorenzaccio (Acte V, scène 6).

UN LIEU ÉCLATÉ

Dans *Lorenzaccio*, Musset applique donc une certaine unité d'action, interprétée, il est vrai, dans un sens large, comme la résultante d'éléments convergents. La plupart des systèmes dramatiques s'y conforment d'ailleurs, contraints qu'ils sont de se plier aux nécessités de la représentation qui ne dispose que d'un temps limité et d'une attention relative des spectateurs.

Une telle concentration est loin d'apparaître dans le traitement du lieu. Bien au contraire, l'action de la pièce est marquée par un éclatement local qui aboutit à une multiplicité de décors.

Lorenzaccio se déroule dans cinq lieux principaux différents : 32 scènes se situent à Florence, 1 à Montolivet, près de Florence, 2 à la campagne, 2 à Venise, 1 dans une auberge. 20 décors sont utilisés, 11 décors extérieurs et 9 décors d'intérieur.

Les 11 décors extérieurs sont le cadre de 17 scènes : une rue (5 scènes), une place (2 scènes), le bord de l'Arno (2 scènes), un jardin (1 scène), une cour du palais du duc (1 scène), le parvis de l'église de Montolivet (1 scène), le portail d'une église (1 scène), une rue située devant le palais du duc (1 scène), une vallée (1 scène), une plaine (1 scène), la grande place de Florence (1 scène).

Les 9 décors d'intérieur intéressent 21 scènes : 4 scènes pour le palais du duc ; 4 scènes pour le palais Strozzi ; 2 scènes pour les appartements du marquis ; 2 scènes pour les appartements de la marquise ; 1 scène pour le boudoir de la marquise ; 3 scènes pour la chambre de Lorenzaccio ; 2 scènes pour le palais Soderini ; 2 scènes pour le cabinet de Philippe à Venise ; 1 scène pour une auberge.

Cette ouverture spatiale s'inscrit dans une conception théâtrale d'ensemble. Elle est d'abord la conséquence directe de la complexité de l'action qui rend nécessaire une spécificité des lieux : les différents complots ne peuvent en effet se dérouler dans le lieu unique cher aux classiques. Elle est ensuite la manifestation de ce pittoresque qu'affectionnent les romantiques. Ils refusent de privilégier certaines réalités au détriment d'autres, s'appliquent à décrire la vie dans toute son ouverture et toute sa richesse : les décors sont indiqués avec une précision minutieuse, les accessoires ne manquent pas, les attitudes sont fidèlement rendues.

Cet éclatement spatial permet enfin, en faisant se succéder décors extérieurs et décors intérieurs, de jouer habilement sur le contraste entre les mouvements de foule et les scènes intimes : l'apaisement souvent mélancolique suit ainsi l'agitation de la rue (Acte I, scène 3 ; Acte I, scène 2) ; les soubresauts collectifs font ainsi place aux troubles de l'âme (Acte IV, scène 5 ; Acte IV, scène 6). Une telle conception, reposant sur le désir de rendre compte d'un contexte historique, jointe à la multiplicité des intrigues, explique par ailleurs l'importance de la distribution : quarante personnages, plusieurs dizaines de figurants, voilà qui aide encore à l'émergence du pittoresque et à l'animation du spectacle.

UNE DURÉE DE DIX JOURS

Malgré certaines imprécisions de la part de Musset qui ne se soucie guère, semble-t-il, de souligner la succession temporelle, il est possible de situer dans le temps le déroulement de la pièce. L'action occupe dix journées : elle est donc relativement ramassée, beaucoup plus que dans la réalité historique, ce qui témoigne d'une certaine volonté de concentrer les faits. Une série d'indications disséminées tout au long de l'œuvre permettent de reconstituer la marche des événements.

Du 29 décembre 1535 au 7 janvier 1536.

- Le marchand le précise à la scène 5 de l'Acte V : le duc a été assassiné « l'an 1536 », « le 6 du mois », « à six heures de la nuit ». Les données historiques ajoutent : en janvier et rectifient : en 1537.

- L'élection de Côme de Médicis, qui termine la pièce, a lieu le lendemain, c'est-à-dire le 7 janvier, puisque, le matin qui suit le meurtre, Corsi répond à une question de Niccolini : « Côme sera ici dans la matinée de demain (...) « (Acte V, scène 1).

- L'aveu de la marquise à son mari, à la scène 4 de l'Acte IV, se situe la veille du meurtre du duc, donc le 5 janvier. Il prend place en effet immédiatement après les recommandations de Lorenzo à Scoronconcolo de la scène 3 : « (...) ne manque pas de venir à minuit (...) ».

- Or, le marquis Cibo est de retour après une absence d'une semaine qu'il annonce, juste avant son départ, à la scène 3 de l'Acte I : « ce sera l'affaire d'une semaine ».

- L'Acte I se déroule donc le 29 décembre, qui plus est, un vendredi, comme le signale une femme en faisant allusion au pèlerinage de Montolivet : « (...) je n'y viens jamais qu'un seul vendredi » (Acte I, scène 5).

- L'action s'ouvre, par conséquent, le vendredi 29 décembre 1535, pour s'achever le dimanche 7 janvier 1536.

La succession des événements

Dans les détails, voici quelle pourrait être la succession des événements :

Acte I, scène 1 : le début du vendredi 29 décembre 1535 (le duc : « Il est minuit (...) »).
Scène 2 : l'aube (une indication scénique précise : « Le point du jour »).
Scènes 3, 4 et 5 : dans la journée.
Scène 6 : le soir de ce même vendredi (Catherine : « Le soleil commence à baisser »).

Acte II, scène 1 : le même jour, à la fin de la journée (Léon Strozzi raconte en effet l'incident de la foire de Montolivet et Pierre avertit : « Allons dîner, le dîner est servi »).
Situer la scène 2 de l'Acte II qui marque une rupture temporelle par rapport à la scène 1 est plus délicat, mais possible.

Dans la scène qui suit, la marquise se prépare à recevoir, pour la première fois, le duc. Or, le jour de l'arrivée de son mari, c'est-à-dire le 5 janvier, le cardinal lui reprochera : « Il ne faut pas une grande science, pour garder un amant un peu plus de trois jours » (Acte IV,scène 4).

La scène 3 de l'Acte II se situe donc le mardi 2 janvier, de même que, probablement, la scène qui précède.

Les scènes 4, 5, 6 et 7 de l'Acte II sont liées par la continuité temporelle : Lorenzo se déplace en effet successivement du palais Soderini au palais Strozzi, puis au palais ducal. Un jour a passé : la scène 6 montre Tebaldeo en train de faire le portrait du duc, alors que Lorenzo, à la scène 2 de l'Acte II, disait au peintre : « Viens demain à mon palais (...) ». Nous voici donc le mercredi 3 janvier. C'est la nuit (Philippe : « Voilà la nuit », scène 5).

L'acte III prend place le jeudi 4 janvier. Lorenzo, qui fait allusion à ses projets d'assassinat dont la réalisation aura lieu le 6 janvier, s'exclame : « (...) dans deux jours, les hommes comparaîtront devant le tribunal de ma volonté » (scène 3).

Au matin, Lorenzo se livre à son combat simulé avec Scoronconcolo (scène 1), Pierre regrette l'échec de son action (scène 2) et se fait arrêter (scène 3), tandis que Catherine et Marie déplorent l'attitude de Lorenzo (scène 4).

Acte III, scènes 5 et 6 : la fin de la matinée (la marquise : « Il est midi passé », scène 6).

Acte III, scène 7 : de nouveau, le soir (une indication scénique signale : « Les quarante Strozzi, à souper »).

L'acte IV s'ouvre le lendemain, vendredi 5 janvier, puisque Lorenzo précise à la scène 1, à propos du duc : « Ce soir, je l'emmène chez moi (...) » . Ce doit être le matin et les scènes 2, 3, 4, 5 et 6, se succèdent tout au long de la journée.

Acte IV, scènes 7 et 8 : le soir (Lorenzo : « Voici le soleil qui se couche », scène 7).

Acte IV, scène 9 : c'est la nuit (une indication scénique signale : « il est nuit »).

Acte IV, scènes 10 et 11 : au cours de la nuit du 6 janvier (après le souper du duc de la scène 10, intervient le meurtre de la scène 11 qui a lieu à six heures du matin, le 6 janvier).

L'acte V s'ouvre le matin du 6 janvier, avec, à la scène 1, l'annonce de l'assassinat du duc.

Scène 2 : arrivée, l'après-midi, de Lorenzo à Venise.

Scènes 3 et 4 : au cours de la même journée, discussion de Pierre avec le messager de François 1er et commentaires, à Florence, sur la mort d'Alexandre.

La scène 5 de l'acte V se déroule le lendemain matin, le dimanche 7. En effet, l'orfèvre précise : « Le Côme arrive aujourd'hui (...) », et cette arrivée avait été annoncée à la scène 1 de l'Acte V pour le 7 au matin. Les deux dernières scènes prennent place le même jour, la mort de Lorenzaccio de la scène 6 ayant été considérablement avancée par Musset, puisqu'elle se situe, en réalité, le 26 février 1548.

Action unifiée, mais complexe ; éclatement spatial contribuant à créer le pittoresque ; multiplicité des personnages ; subtil dosage faisant se succéder mouvements de foule et scènes d'intérieur ; resserrement temporel relatif, la construction de *Lorenzaccio* est marquée par le romantisme, mais par un romantisme maîtrisé, dominé, qui ne tombe pas dans les excès de la tradition naissante du drame français.

TABLEAU RÉCAPITULATIF I : lieu, temps, action

Actes	Sc.	Lieux	Temps	Lorenzo (17 scènes)	
I	1	un jardin	29 décembre minuit	dessein dissimulé	
	2	une rue	29 décembre l'aube		
	3	palais Cibo (chez le marquis)	29 décembre journée		
	4	palais ducal (une cour)	29 décembre journée	dessein soupçonné	
	5	Montolivet (l'église)	29 décembre journée		
	6	l'Arno	29 décembre le soir		**EXPOSITION**
II	1	palais Strozzi	29 décembre le soir		
	2	une église	2 janvier	dessein annoncé	
	3	palais Cibo (chez la marquise)	2 janvier		
	4	palais Soderini	3 janvier le soir	dessein annoncé	
	5	palais Strozzi	3 janvier le soir	dessein annoncé	
	6	palais ducal	3 janvier le soir	le vol de la cotte de mailles ACTION	
	7	une rue (devant le palais ducal)	3 janvier le soir		

Les Strozzi (15 scènes)		La marquise (6 scènes)	Le peuple (9 scènes)
Philippe (11 scènes)	**Pierre** (12 scènes)		
Louise insultée	Louise insultée		mécontentement EXPOSITION
		intrigue avec le duc EXPOSITION	
provocation de Salviati	provocation de Salviati		contestation
les bannis	les bannis		bannissement
patience	colère		
		confession	
prudence	vengeance		
	Salviati réchappe (coup de théâtre)		

EXPOSITION (Les Strozzi)

ACTION (Les Strozzi)

EXPOSITION (La marquise)

ACTION (La marquise)

ACTION (Le peuple)

TABLEAU RÉCAPITULATIF II : lieu, temps, action

Actes	Sc.	Lieux	Temps	Lorenzo (17 scènes)
III	1	chambre de Lorenzo	4 janvier le matin	dessein révélé exposition
	2	palais Strozzi	4 janvier le matin	
	3	une rue	4 janvier le matin	dessein confirmé
	4	palais Soderini	4 janvier le matin	
	5	palais Cibo (chez la marquise)	4 janvier midi	
	6	boudoir Cibo	4 janvier midi	
	7	palais Strozzi	4 janvier le soir	
IV	1	palais ducal	5 janvier le matin	le piège coup de théâtre
	2	une rue	5 janvier la journée	
	3	une rue	5 janvier la journée	préparatifs
	4	palais Cibo (chez le marquis)	5 janvier la journée	
	5	chambre de Lorenzo	5 janvier la journée	préparatifs
	6	une vallée	5 janvier la journée	

ACTION

Les Strozzi (15 scènes)		La marquise (6 scènes)	Le peuple (9 scènes)
Philippe (11 scènes)	**Pierre** (12 scènes)		
ralliement à l'action	complot		
découragement	arrestation coup de théâtre		protestation
		l'attente	
		le rendez-vous	
mort de Louise : désespoir coup de théâtre			
	mort de Louise : fureur		
		l'aveu au mari DÉNOUEMENT 1	
rupture : « mains propres » DÉNOUEMENT 1	rupture : « mains sales » DÉNOUEMENT 1		

ACTION

ACTION

ACTION

TABLEAU RÉCAPITULATIF III : lieu, temps, action

Actes	Sc.	Lieux	Temps	Lorenzo (17 scènes)	
	7	l'Arno	5 janvier le soir	avertissement aux républicains coup de théâtre	
	8	une plaine	5 janvier le soir		ACTION
	9	une place	5 janvier la nuit	préparatifs	
	10	palais ducal	6 janvier la nuit	avertissement au duc coup de théâtre	
	11	chambre de Lorenzo	6 janvier 6 h du matin	assassinat du duc **DÉNOUEMENT 1**	
V	1	palais ducal	6 janvier le matin		
	2	Venise : chez Philippe	6 janvier après-midi	poursuivi	
	3	une rue	6 janvier après-midi		
	4	une auberge	6 janvier après-midi		DÉNOUEMENT 2
	5	une place	7 janvier le matin		
	6	Venise : chez Philippe	7 janvier la journée	mort	
	7	Florence : la grande place	7 janvier la journée		

Les Strozzi (15 scènes)			
Philippe (11 scènes)	**Pierre** (12 scènes)	**La marquise** (6 scènes)	**Le peuple** (9 scènes)
			insouciance coup de théâtre
	compromission avec François 1er		
			la succession
retraite			
		le pardon DÉNOUEMENT 2	
	ambition		
			bavardages
résignation			assassinat de Lorenzaccio DÉNOUEMENT 1
			élection de Côme DÉNOUEMENT 2

DÉNOUEMENT 2

ACTION

6 | La peinture des personnages

DES ÊTRES HABITÉS PAR MUSSET

Il a souvent été reproché à Musset de n'avoir pas su caractériser suffisamment les personnages[1] qu'il a mis en scène. Cette accusation est en partie fondée : il a tendance à leur transmettre ses états d'âme, à en faire ses porte-parole, ou à exprimer, à travers eux, les multiples facettes d'une vision du monde complexe. Cette façon que l'auteur de *Lorenzaccio* a de vivre intensément dans chacune de ses créations explique le lyrisme qui les anime et la sincérité qui en émane. Il leur a prêté son style somptueux et sensible, il leur a légué ses problèmes personnels dont il est littéralement obsédé. Aussi, malgré leurs préocupations et leurs caractères différents, les personnages ne cessent de s'exprimer à la manière de Musset.

Se ressemblant stylistiquement comme des frères, ils pourraient néanmoins être solidement campés, grâce aux modalités spécifiques de leur existence et aux visions du monde dissemblables qui régissent leur vie. Mais ce n'est pas le but que poursuit Musset. C'est davantage à la valeur collective de ses personnages qu'à leur signification individuelle qu'il s'intéresse. Il se contente donc souvent de les silhouetter : il en fait des symboles, des représentants significatifs d'une attitude, d'un comportement.

---

1. Les personnages de la pièce ayant une fonction essentiellement symbolique, leur analyse est largement complétée dans les chapitres 7 (« Les grands thèmes », cf. p. 51), et 8 (« *Lorenzaccio* et le mal du siècle romantique », cf. p. 65) auxquels on se reportera.

LORENZACCIO, OU LA DIFFICULTÉ DE VIVRE

Le personnage central de Lorenzaccio a toutes les caractéristiques du héros romantique. Il en a le physique. C'est un être frêle, fragile, dont la vie de débauche n'a pas totalement fané une grâce un peu féminine. C'est un séducteur, écartelé entre les aspirations à l'idéal et l'attirance pour les plaisirs, une sorte d'ange déchu qui garde la nostalgie de l'innocence perdue.

Toute sa morale, tout son comportement sont marqués par cette contradiction. Il est tourné vers le beau et vers le bien, mais constate avec horreur que ce ne sont guère là des valeurs terrestres. Il en éprouve un grand désespoir. Il témoigne de ce mal du siècle, de cette difficulté d'être d'une génération romantique consciente de l'absurdité du monde, de la perversion de l'homme. Il a utilisé la débauche pour approcher Alexandre de Médicis, afin de pouvoir mieux le tuer et ainsi atteindre le but qu'il s'est fixé. Mais les plaisirs lui sont devenus peu à peu indispensables : ce sont maintenant pour lui des moyens d'évasion destinés à lui faire oublier son irrémédiable déchéance.

Lorenzaccio est un jeune homme pur et tranquille qui, brusquement saisi par le spectacle de l'impuissance et de la médiocrité humaines, a entrepris de régénérer cette humanité. Il est décidé à agir seul, envers et contre tout, envers et contre tous, à utiliser tous les moyens pour parvenir à ses fins. Il est résolu à lancer un véritable défi au monde. Mais il succombe sous l'ampleur d'une tâche surhumaine. Il s'écroule, miné par la démesure de son dessein, contesté par les procédés qu'il est contraint d'utiliser, finalement tué par l'inutilité de son geste. Il sait, à l'avance, dans quelle impasse il s'est engagé, il le dit avec une lucidité amère : « Je voulais agir seul, sans le secours d'aucun homme. Je travaillais pour l'humanité ; mais mon orgueil restait solitaire au milieu de tous mes rêves philanthropiques (...). Je ne voulais pas soulever les masses, ni conquérir la gloire bavarde d'un paralytique comme Cicéron. Je voulais (...) porter mon épée sanglante sur la tribune, et laisser la fumée du sang d'Alexandre monter au nez des harangueurs, pour réchauffer leur cervelle ampoulée (...). Tout ce que j'ai à voir, moi, c'est que je suis perdu, et que les hommes n'en profiteront pas plus qu'ils me comprendront » (Acte III, scène 3).

FLORENCE, UNE « VILLE-PERSONNAGE »

Face à Lorenzaccio, le personnage le plus important, c'est Florence. La ville est l'enjeu du combat engagé. Elle est au centre de la lutte menée entre les partisans de la liberté et ceux de la tyrannie. Elle est l'objet de toutes les convoitises, le siège du beau et du laid, du bien et du mal, elle suscite l'amour et la haine.

Musset s'est plu à la décrire dans toute sa complexité. Il en fait un être vivant, un être de chair. La ville est au cœur de sa pièce. Ce n'est pas surprenant chez ce romantique qui se sentait en communion avec la Renaissance italienne. Mais il s'agit d'une Renaissance italienne transposée, repensée, dont les caractères sont accentués, les contrastes forcés. Cet appel venu du sud, auquel répond toute une génération, revêt une signification véritablement symbolique : partir pour l'Italie, c'est rechercher la luminosité de cieux toujours bleus ; c'est aspirer à une vie libre, sans contrainte ; c'est se plonger dans les délices de l'art ; c'est se retremper dans une civilisation dont on admire le raffinement, et dont on se défend à peine de ressentir la cruauté avec une délectation morbide, cette cruauté qui témoigne d'un accomplissement sans frein des désirs, d'une exaltation dans la démesure.

C'est cette vision que Musset essaie de faire passer. Une contradiction secondaire, mais significative, témoigne de ce véritable envoûtement, de cette image d'Épinal que l'Italie représente pour lui : l'action se déroule en hiver (du 29 décembre au 7 janvier). Le climat de Florence n'a rien de méditerranéen. Certes, quelques indications, qui témoignent d'un souci de vérité, viennent le souligner (le duc : « Il fait un froid de tous les diables », Acte I, scène 1 ; premier écolier : « Mon portefeuille me glace les mains », Acte I, scène 2 ; la marquise : « L'hiver est si long ! », Acte I, scène 3). Mais l'ambiance générale est ensoleillée et évoque l'été : le duc Alexandre reçoit ses visiteurs sur une terrasse (Acte I, scène 4) ; la foule converse devant l'église de Saint-Miniato (Acte I, scène 5) ; l'orfèvre et le marchand s'entretiennent, assis en plein air (Acte V, scène 5).

En fait, si Musset part de données réelles, son imagination ne cesse de les transformer, de les interpréter. Ainsi multiplie-t-il les évocations d'un peuple coloré. Ainsi éprouve-t-il le besoin d'évoquer fugitivement des figures historiques de l'époque comme celle de « ce hâbleur de Cellini », le célèbre sculpteur (Acte I, scène 5), et de camper beaucoup plus longuement le peintre Telbadeo Freccia qui expose sa conception de l'art (Acte II, scène 2). Ainsi s'efforce-t-il de marquer les oppositions entre les prétentions de raffinement du duc, qui se manifestent par un goût barbare du faste, et son mépris de l'art (« Je protège les arts comme un autre, et j'ai chez moi les premiers artistes de l'Italie ; mais je n'entends rien au respect du pape pour ces statues qu'il excommunierait demain, si elles étaient en chair et en os », Acte I, scène 4).

DES CONSTRUCTIONS LOURDES DE SYMBOLES

Toute cette cohorte de personnages qui gravite autour de Lorenzaccio et de Florence est également lourde de valeurs symboliques.

Alexandre de Médicis, avec son langage élémentaire, avec son comportement instinctif, c'est l'appétit de plaisir, la recherche fruste de la jouissance immédiate, le désir de vivre dans l'instant, la cruauté inconsciente d'un être tout de chair (« Mais qu'est-ce que je fais donc de si mal ? Je vaux bien mes voisins ; je vaux, ma foi, mieux que le pape », rétorque-t-il à la marquise qui lui reproche son action politique (Acte III, scène 6).

Philippe, c'est la réflexion stérile, l'idéalisme improductif (« Qu'il t'est facile à toi, dans le silence du cabinet, de tracer d'une main légère une ligne mince et pure comme un cheveu sur ce papier blanc ! », reconnaît-il lui-même, à la scène 1 de l'Acte II).

Pierre, c'est l'activisme irresponsable (« Un bon coup de lancette guérit tous les maux », répond-il aux objections de son père, à la scène 2 de l'Acte III).

Le cardinal, c'est la satisfaction tirée de l'intrigue, la joie sombre d'éprouver sa puissance occulte (« (...) je serai l'anneau invisible qui l'[le duc] attachera, pieds et poings liés, à la chaîne de fer dont Rome et César tiennent les deux bouts », exulte-t-il, à la scène 3 de l'Acte II).

Catherine, c'est l'innocence intacte (« Il ne l'aime plus ? Ah ! comment peut-on offrir sans honte un cœur pareil ! », dit-elle à propos du duc, Acte III, scène 4).

Marie, c'est la souffrance résignée (« Mais tout ce que je vois m'entraîne vers la tombe », confie-t-elle à Catherine, à la scène 4 de l'Acte III).

Tebaldeo, c'est le refus de la compromission, l'aspiration à une liberté noble et fière (« Je n'appartiens à personne », oppose-t-il aux propositions de Lorenzaccio, à la scène 2 de l'acte II).

Giomo, c'est la cruauté aveugle, la force brute (« Quand mon Giomo frappe, il frappe ferme », remarque le duc, à la scène 6 de l'Acte II).

Scoronconcolo, c'est la fidélité presque instinctive (« Pour toi, je remettrais le Christ en croix », explique-t-il à Lorenzaccio, à la scène 1 de l'acte III).

Pièce d'une grande complexité de construction, œuvre toute bruissante de symboles, *Lorenzaccio* est riche d'une autre richesse : les thèmes se succèdent, se mêlent souvent, montrant, une fois encore, l'ampleur de la réflexion, des préoccupations et des interrogations de Musset.

LA RELATIVITÉ DES CHOIX RELIGIEUX ET MORAUX

A de multiples reprises, dans *Lorenzaccio*, apparaissent des positions diverses face à la religion et à la morale. Musset en dresse comme le panorama : il expose ainsi le fruit de ses hésitations, sa difficulté à opérer un choix.

Une religion pervertie

Dans ce domaine, les personnages de la pièce adoptent des attitudes variées. Une première distinction s'impose : alors que Musset ne porte pas de jugements de valeur sur les laïcs, il est beaucoup plus sévère pour le clergé : son rôle dirigeant et les conséquences morales que ses perversions peuvent avoir lui confèrent une grande responsabilité, et rendent particulièrement dangereuses ses actions contestables. Il s'attaque violemment aux ministres du culte. Ce qu'il reproche au pape, c'est son intervention dans le domaine temporel, alors qu'il ne devrait jouer qu'un rôle spirituel (Acte I, scène 2) ; c'est aussi son immoralité qui ne l'empêche pas de vouloir donner des leçons aux autres (Acte I, scène 4). Ce qu'il réprouve chez le cardinal Cibo, c'est l'utilisation hypocrite qu'il fait de ses fonctions pour satisfaire son goût de l'intrigue (Acte II, scène 3) ; c'est également la perte de tout sens moral qui, au mépris de la personne humaine, l'amène à considérer que tous les moyens sont bons : détournement de correspondance, malgré les protestations d'Agnolo (« Hélas ! Éminence, c'est un péché », Acte I, scène 3) ; excuse du geste sacrilège du duc (Acte I, scène 3) ; véritable chantage à la confession (Acte II, scène 3) ; appel à la prostitution (Acte IV, scène 4).

Certes, quelques ecclésiastiques demeurent dans le droit chemin, comme Valori, homme intègre (le duc lui adresse ce compliment, à la scène 4 de l'Acte 1 : « Vous êtes, pardieu, le seul prêtre honnête homme que j'aie vu de ma vie »), ou comme le prieur, tout de bonté (voir son attitude conciliante, à la scène I de l'Acte II).

Mais, de façon générale, on assiste à une dégénérescence de la foi et à une dénaturation de la morale. La religion tombe dans la superstition (voir les explications du marchand qui place la mort du duc sous le signe du chiffre six, Acte V, scène 5). Elle n'est plus qu'un prétexte à réjouissances (voir le pèlerinage de Montolivet qui est devenu davantage l'occasion d'une foire qu'un acte de piété, Acte I, scène 5) ou à spectacles (Acte II, scène 2). Affaiblie, elle a perdu sa capacité à défendre les valeurs morales (Acte I, scène 1).

Des attitudes multiples devant la foi

Dans ces conditions, la religion n'a plus cette unité qui faisait sa force. Elle ne peut empêcher la multiplication des interprétations divergentes du monde. Et la pièce éclate en attitudes multiples devant la foi, sur lesquelles Musset se garde bien de porter jugement : est-ce le duc qui a raison dans son refus des pratiques religieuses (« Toi qui ne vas pas à la messe (...) », lui reproche la marquise, Acte III, scène 6) ? Est-ce plutôt la marquise, dans son déisme (« (...) es-tu sûr que l'Éternité soit sourde, et qu'il n'y ait pas un écho de la vie dans le séjour hideux des trépassés ? Sais-tu où vont les larmes des peuples, quand le vent les emporte ? », dit-elle au duc, à la scène 6 de l'Acte III) ? Philippe serait-il dans le vrai, avec sa conception d'un Dieu injuste (« Dieu de justice ! Dieu de justice ! que t'ai-je fait ? », proteste-t-il, à la scène 7 de l'Acte III) ? ou serait-ce Pierre, avec sa vision d'un Dieu de vengeance (« Écoutez-moi, prêtres ; si vous êtes l'image de Dieu, vous pouvez recevoir un serment. Par tout ce qu'il y a d'instruments de supplice sous le ciel, par les tortures de l'Enfer... », (Acte IV, scène 2) ? Que choisir ? Lorenzaccio et son attitude de défi (« Ma vie entière est au bout de ma dague, et que la Providence retourne ou non la tête, en m'entendant frapper, je jette la nature humaine à pile ou face sur la tombe d'Alexandre (...) », Acte III, scène 3) ? Tebaldeo et son assimilation de la religion à l'art (« Le chant de l'orgue me révèle leur pensée, et me fait pénétrer dans leur âme », dit-il en parlant des œuvres de Raphaël et de Michel-Ange, « je regarde les personnages de leurs tableaux si saintement agenouillés, et j'écoute, comme si les cantiques du chœur sortaient de leurs bouches entrouvertes (...) », Acte II, scène 2) ? ou encore Catherine et sa saisie intuitive d'orientation panthéiste (« Que le ciel est beau ! que tout cela est vaste et tranquille ! comme Dieu est partout ! », s'extasie-t-elle, à la scène 6 de l'Acte I) ? C'est à chacun de décider selon ses aspirations et ses états d'âme.

LE JEU DES APPARENCES ET DE LA RÉALITÉ

Un monde d'illusions

Cette absence de détermination morale est la conséquence d'une vision globale du monde vérifiée par les données cruelles de l'expérience : la vie est faite de revirements . Le hasard y est tout-puissant ; aucune stabilité n'y est assurée ; aucune sécurité n'y existe. Voilà qui incite à voir dans l'univers l'empire du relatif, le théâtre des transformations, où se déroule le ballet jamais achevé des apparences et de la réalité.

Lorenzaccio est dominé par l'illusion. Son triomphe est particulièrement net, lorqu'elle échappe à la volonté de l'homme, lorsqu'elle se développe en marge de l'action humaine. Témoignage alors d'un monde qui est par nature faux-semblant, elle se manifeste dans les rêves ou dans les transcriptions cauchemardesques faites à l'état de veille. C'est une illusion bien ambiguë, puisqu'elle constitue à la fois une prémonition de faits réels et une distorsion de cette réalité qui se trouve comme accentuée, comme transfigurée par ces évocations aux images somptueuses, quelque peu comparables aux interprétations du quotidien par l'art.

Une réalité ambiguë

Le songe se manifeste comme le pendant de l'existence de tous les jours à laquelle il vient donner un éclairage différent, conférer une dimension nouvelle. Il apparaît presque plus réel que la réalité soumise à l'ambiguïté.

Ainsi Maffio, après s'être éveillé de son cauchemar : « Il me semblait dans mon rêve voir ma sœur traverser notre jardin, tenant une lanterne sourde, et couverte de pierreries. Je me suis éveillé en sursaut. Dieu sait que ce n'est qu'une illusion, mais une illusion trop forte pour que le sommeil ne s'enfuie pas devant elle », découvre une réalité aussi effrayante : « Suis-je éveillé ? c'est le fantôme de ma sœur, il tient une lanterne sourde et un collier brillant étincelle sur sa poitrine aux rayons de la lune » (Acte I, scène 1).

Ainsi l'hallucination de Marie, évoquant son fils, ce « pauvre enfant vêtu de noir » qui réapparaîtra plus tard dans l'œuvre poétique de Musset (*la Nuit de Décembre*), constitue une matérialisation du déchirement de Lorenzo : « J'ai entendu tout d'un coup marcher lentement dans la galerie ; je me suis retournée, un homme vêtu de noir venait à moi, un livre sous le bras : c'était toi, Renzo : « Comme tu reviens de bonne heure ! », me suis-je écriée. Mais le spectre s'est assis auprès de la lampe, sans me répondre ; il a ouvert son livre, et j'ai reconnu mon Lorenzino d'autrefois » (Acte II, scène 4).

Ainsi la transposition de Lorenzo, décrivant sa vie, représente une vision concrète, beaucoup plus réelle que ne pourrait l'être la liste de ses turpitudes : « Mais moi, pendant ce temps-là, j'ai plongé ; je me suis enfoncé dans cette mer houleuse de la vie ; j'en ai parcouru toutes les profondeurs, couvert de ma cloche de verre ; tandis que vous admiriez la surface, j'ai vu les débris des naufrages, les ossements et les Léviathans » (Acte III, scène 3).

LE TRIOMPHE DU MASQUE

Des visages masqués

L'importance du rêve soulignait le rôle joué par les apparences. Le thème du masque montre l'ampleur des dissimulations qui marquent les personnages. Le masque est omniprésent. Il apparaît concrètement durant les fêtes et s'accompagne du déguisement : travestis, masqués au sens propre du terme, les Florentins peuvent ainsi dissimuler leur identité et se livrer, en toute liberté, à leur fantaisie, à leurs impulsions. Paradoxalement, le masque leur permet, en fait, de libérer leur être profond, d'échapper à leur être social. Dès le début de la pièce, à la scène 2 de l'Acte I, Musset représente ces réjouissances, occasions de faire triompher, à la faveur du masque, l'instinct sur la raison, l'inconscient sur le conscient.

Le jeu dangereux de la dissimulation

Mais plus profondément, les personnages ne se contentent pas de masquer leur visage ; ils masquent aussi leur caractère. Les apparences qu'ils plaquent sur leur vraie personnalité concourent parfois à leur propre aveuglement. Comme ils ne peuvent s'avouer une réalité contraire à leurs aspirations, ils l'escamotent, en ayant recours à des explications plus satisfaisantes. C'est de cette auto-intoxication qu'est notamment victime la marquise Cibo, lorsqu'elle essaie de se persuader que sa passion pour Alexandre est due à de hauts motifs politiques (« Et pourquoi est-ce que tu te mêles à tout cela, toi, Florence ? Qui est-ce donc que j'aime ? Est-ce toi ? Est-ce lui ? », s'interroge-t-elle, à la scène 3 de l'Acte II). Bindo et Venturi ont un comportement semblable, lorsqu'ils tentent de se cacher à eux-mêmes la satisfaction que leur procurent les faveurs du duc (« C'est un tour infâme », « Cela est terrible ! », se lamentent-ils hypocritement, à la scène 4 de l'Acte II).

Parfois, les faux-semblants ont pour but d'égarer l'entourage. L'exemple le plus significatif est évidemment fourni par Lorenzo qui ne cesse de réfréner ses aspirations profondes, en leur imposant le masque de la débauche. Lorenzo, c'est l'être qui se contraint à jouer un rôle, qui tourne résolument le dos à sa véritable nature, pour la remplacer par une apparence factice, artificielle (« Pour plaire à mon cousin, il fallait arriver à lui porté par les larmes des familles ; pour devenir son ami et acquérir sa confiance, il fallait baiser sur ses lèvres épaisses tous les restes de ses orgies. J'étais pur comme un lis, et cependant je n'ai pas reculé devant cette tâche », confie-t-il à Philippe Strozzi, à la scène 3 de l'Acte III).

Voilà qui aboutit à une dépersonnalisation, à une mutilation de l'être, à un morcellement de la personnalité écartelée entre la vérité et les apparences. Et Lorenzaccio constate lucidement : « (...) moi, qui n'ai voulu prendre qu'un masque pareil à leurs (les débauchés) visages, je ne puis ni me retrouver moi-même, ni laver mes mains, même avec du sang ! » (Acte IV, scène 5).

Cette ambiguïté de la réalité aboutit à une cohabitation de tendances diverses, voire opposées : elle se trouve concrétisée, d'une manière caractéristique, par les différents noms que reçoit le personnage principal tout au cours de la pièce : « Lorenzo de Médicis » (le duc, Acte I, scène 4), c'est le nom prestigieux du descendant d'une famille noble, « Lorenzino » (Marie, Acte II, scène 4), c'est le nom tendre utilisé pour l'enfant d'autrefois, « Renzino » (le duc, Acte II, scène 4), c'est le surnom trop familier donné au compagnon de débauche, « Lorenzetta » (le duc, Acte I, scène 4), c'est le diminutif ambigu qui convient à l'être efféminé, « Lorenzaccio » (Lorenzo, acte III, scène 3), c'est le terme péjoratif qui s'applique à l'individu dangereux maudit par les gens honnêtes. Que de masques placés tour à tour sur les visages ! Que de personnalités successivement endossées ! Quel risque encouru d'y laisser son identité !

Lorenzaccio, à jouer avec les masques, y perdra son âme. Mais il n'est pas le seul à baigner dans cet océan de contradictions. Les autres, simplement, parviennent, semble-t-il, à mieux concilier l'inconciliable. Dans cet exercice, le cardinal Cibo est passé maître : chez lui, l'hypocrisie et le cynisme font apparemment bon ménage avec les convictions religieuses.

L'ALLIANCE DU LUXE ET DE LA CRUAUTÉ

Le faste, la pompe, le luxe, c'est un autre domaine qui permet à l'illusion de donner toute sa mesure. Mener une existence raffinée, se prétendre protecteur des arts, attirer à sa cour des peintres éminents, s'entourer d'un décor somptueux, s'habiller de vêtements aux étoffes les plus rares, voilà qui permet au duc de Florence de dissimuler son vide intellectuel et sa cruauté de barbare, sous le voile d'apparences plus satisfaisantes.

La scène 6 de l'Acte II souligne particulièrement ce jeu d'oppositions. Après avoir fait ce commentaire cruel : « Quand je suis en pointe de gaieté, tous mes moindres coups sont mortels », le duc émet cette remarque esthétique : « Cela vaut toujours mieux, d'ailleurs, de poser le col découvert ; regarde les antiques [1] ». De même, la référence martiale du duc, lorsqu'il justifie son habitude de porter une cotte de mailles : « Ce n'est pas que je me défie de personne ; comme tu dis, c'est une habitude, — pure habitude de soldat » contraste avec la description somptueuse de Lorenzaccio : « Votre habit est magnifique. Quel parfum que ces gants ! ».

LES AMBIGUÏTÉS DE L'AMOUR ET DE LA FEMME

L'amour et la femme se situent au cœur même des contradictions qui divisent l'être humain. Musset en parle en connaisseur ; la passion a en effet joué un rôle essentiel dans sa vie : ses multiples expériences amoureuses ont contribué à affiner sa sensibilité, l'ont aidé à quitter cette existence superficielle de dandy qui était la sienne au sortir de l'adolescence, et lui ont permis, grâce aux leçons de la douleur, de devenir pleinement homme et pleinement créateur :

> « L'homme est un apprenti ; la douleur est son maître.
> Et nul ne se connaît, tant qu'il n'a pas souffert [2] ».

---

1. *Les antiques* : les œuvres d'art de l'Antiquité.
2. *Nuit d'octobre* (1837)

L'amour, malgré les désillusions que son goût de la pose exagère souvent, est donc considéré par Musset comme l'accomplissement de l'homme, comme sa principale raison de vivre :

« Après avoir souffert, il faut souffrir encore ;
Il faut aimer sans cesse, après avoir aimé[1] ».

Constantes et contradictions

C'est ce qui explique la place primordiale occupée par la femme dans son œuvre, et plus particulièrement dans *Lorenzaccio*. Elle y apparaît comme un être multiple. Mais, malgré les différences de caractère et de comportement, elle possède un certain nombre de constantes spécifiques qui en font à la fois le charme et le danger.

La femme, c'est la pudeur (« Tant de pudeur ! », dit Lorenzaccio à propos de Gabrielle, Acte I, scène 1). Mais voilà, il y a l'orgueil, la curiosité ou l'intérêt qui viennent tout balayer (« N'as-tu pas été flattée ? Un amour qui fait l'envie de tant de femmes ! un titre si beau à conquérir, la maîtresse de ... », ironise Lorenzaccio à l'adresse de Catherine, Acte IV, scènes 5 ; « Ah ! pourquoi y a-t-il dans tout cela un aimant, un charme inexplicable qui m'attire ? » s'interroge la marquise, Acte II, scène 3 ; « On me l'a montrée ce soir, sortant du spectacle, dans une robe comme n'en a pas l'impératrice », telle est la description que fait Maffio de sa sœur, Acte 1, scène 6).

La femme, c'est le charme et la beauté (Gabrielle a « deux grands yeux languissants », Acte I, scène 1 ; Louise une « belle épaule (...) toute humide et si fraîche ! », Acte I, scène 2). Mais que d'hypocrisie là-dessous dissimulée (« Voir dans une enfant de quinze ans la rouée à venir », présage Lorenzaccio, Acte 1, scène 1) !

La femme, c'est la sensibilité jamais épuisée (« Mais quel flot violent d'un fleuve magnifique sous cette couche de glace fragile qui craque à chaque pas ! », présage Lorenzaccio de Gabrielle, Acte I, scène 1). Mais que de tentations elle provo-

1. *Nuit d'août* (1836)

que, de combien de perversions elle est la cause (« Quand je pense que cela est, cela me fait l'effet d'une nouvelle qu'on m'apprendrait tout à coup », médite la marquise Cibo, en songeant que c'est son amant qu'elle attend, Acte III, scène 5) !

De la pureté à la débauche

Il y a donc bien une nature profonde de la femme. Mais elle ne doit pas faire oublier la variété des attitudes et des réactions ; elle ne doit pas dissimuler les qualités différentes de sentiments que chacune peut offrir. *Lorenzaccio* en dresse un véritable catalogue.

La femme, ce peut être la courtisane expérimentée que l'on paie argent comptant (Lorenzo à Tebaldeo : « Pourquoi donc ne peux-tu peindre une courtisane, si tu peux peindre un mauvais lieu ? », Acte II, scène 2) ; ou la jeune fille encore pure que l'on débauche, à force de présents et en achetant les parents (exemple type de Gabrielle payée « un millier de ducats » à sa mère, attirée par « un collier brillant », et dont Lorenzaccio affirme : « Jamais arbuste en fleurs n'a promis de fruits plus rares, jamais je n'ai humé dans une atmosphère enfantine plus exquise odeur de courtisanerie », Acte I, scène 1).

La femme, c'est aussi la dame noble avide d'amants admirateurs (première dame : « Il est bête à faire plaisir, ton officier ; que peux-tu faire de cela ? », Acte I, scène 5) ; ou l'oisive succombant à la sensibilité, demandant à la passion la nouveauté et la sensation d'exister (« Advienne que pourra, je veux essayer mon pouvoir », s'écrie la marquise, à la scène 5 de l'Acte III).

La femme, c'est encore la jeune fille sans problème, cherchant dans l'amour l'accord de deux cœurs (Tebaldeo : « Le soir, je vais chez ma maîtresse, et quand la nuit est belle, je la passe sur son balcon », Acte II, scène 2) ; ou l'adolescente, restée pleine de générosité et de fraîcheur, attachée aux vraies valeurs humaines (« Son cœur n'est peut-être pas celui d'un Médicis ; mais, hélas ! c'est encore moins celui d'un honnête homme », regrette Catherine, à propos de Lorenzaccio, Acte I, scène 6).

C'est enfin la vieille femme tendre et résignée (« J'ai trop souffert, ma pauvre Catherine (...). Allons, soutiens-moi, pauvre enfant ; je ne te donnerai pas longtemps cette peine », Acte III, scène 4).

L'amour, ce peut être l'amour sensuel, que l'on prend en passant, et qui n'engage pas (Lorenzo : « J'aurais pleuré avec la première fille que j'ai séduite, si elle ne s'était mise à rire », Acte III, scène 3). Mais ce peut être la passion qui s'empare de tout l'être (la marquise au duc : « Vous autres hommes, cela est si peu pour vous ! Sacrifier le repos de ses jours, la sainte chasteté de l'honneur ! quelquefois ses enfants ; ne vivre que pour un seul être au monde (...) », Acte III, scène 6). Ce peut être aussi un sentiment pur, une affection de sœur, comme chez Catherine qui espère encore en Lorenzaccio (« Je me dis malgré moi que tout n'est pas mort en lui », Acte I, scène 6) ; ou la sollicitude maternelle de Marie qui se souvient de son « Lorenzino d'autrefois » (Acte II, scène 4).

PENSÉE ET ACTION : DES RAPPORTS DIFFICILES

Dans *Lorenzaccio*, se développe aussi une méditation sur la pensée et sur l'action. Ce thème philosophique se trouve puissamment intégré à la pièce dont l'une des principales interrogations porte sur les rapports difficiles qu'entretiennent la réflexion et son application concrète.

La philosophie apparaît, dans *Lorenzaccio*, comme le type même de l'acte gratuit, de la démarche inutile. Musset a construit le personnage de Philippe Strozzi essentiellement en vue de cette démonstration. Le philosophe est un idéaliste, attaché à ses rêves de perfection. Il travaille dans l'absolu : « Que le bonheur des hommes ne soit qu'un rêve, cela est pourtant dur », commente Philippe, à la scène 1 de l'Acte II. Il refuse de regarder la réalité en face : « Arrête ! Ne brise pas comme un roseau mon bâton de vieillesse », répond-il aux propos désabusés de Lorenzaccio, Acte III, scène 3. Il s'épuise à ressasser les mêmes idées stériles : « J'ai trop réfléchi ici-bas ; j'ai trop tourné sur moi-même, comme un cheval de pressoir », constate-t-il, à la scène 3 de l'Acte III. Réduit presque à un enfant, incapable de se déterminer lui-même, il ne peut faire face à l'action et le regrette amèrement : « Mais l'architecte, qui a dans son pupitre des milliers de plans admirables, ne peut soulever de terre le premier pavé de son édifice, quand il vient se mettre à l'ouvrage avec son dos voûté et ses idées obstinées » (Acte II, scène 1).

La contestation de la démarche de Philippe Strozzi par son fils, l'activiste Pierre et par le nihiliste Lorenzaccio, c'est un peu la contestation de la philosophie elle-même. L'échec final du penseur, son renoncement, c'est la reconnaissance des limites de la réflexion. Mais les chemins suivis par Pierre et par Lorenzaccio ne conduisent-ils pas, eux aussi, à la faillite ? Si l'action plonge dans la réalité, elle détruit la pureté des intentions, elle pervertit, elle oblige à se salir les mains.

UN IDÉAL : L'ART

Se réfugier dans le monde des idées ou se lancer dans l'action aboutit donc, dans les deux cas, à une impasse.

Mais, heureusement, il y a l'univers de l'art dans lequel les romantiques ont mis tout leur espoir. Déçus par la réalité, ils s'adonnent à une activité qui, bien qu'elle doive beaucoup au rêve, ne fait pas courir le risque des désillusions, car elle ne vise pas à une transformation, mais à une transposition des données. La somme d'enseignements qu'il est possible de tirer de *Lorenzaccio* permet de se faire une idée assez précise des conceptions artistiques de Musset : les développements qui sont consacrés à ce thème se présentent en effet comme une sorte de dissertation dialoguée. Revers de la médaille, ils sont assez mal liés à l'action principale.

Une nouvelle religion

Sur le plan matériel, Musset pose le problème du mécénat. A s'en rapporter à ces paroles de l'orfèvre : « Si j'étais un grand artiste, j'aimerais les princes, parce qu'eux seuls peuvent faire entreprendre de grands travaux » (Acte I, scène 5), il semble en être partisan. Mais, en fait, sa position est nuancée. L'artiste, pour créer, doit être entièrement libre. Dépendre d'un protecteur risque donc d'avoir des conséquences fâcheuses sur l'activité créatrice (Tebaldeo, le peintre, proclame : « Je n'appartiens à personne. Quand la pensée veut être libre, le corps doit l'être aussi », Acte II, scène 2).

C'est que l'art est une véritable religion, à laquelle il faut se livrer corps et âme. L'artiste est un intermédiaire entre Dieu et les hommes, il témoigne au nom de Dieu d'une vérité. C'est pourquoi Tebaldeo établit des liens très étroits entre les domaines artistique et religieux. Lorsqu'il s'écrie, à propos des chefs-d'œuvre, qu'il ne peut mieux les contempler que dans une église, lorsqu'il ajoute : « (...) des bouffées d'encens aromatiques passent entre eux et moi dans une vapeur légère. Je crois y voir la gloire de l'artiste » (Acte II, scène 2), ce mysticisme, qui fait de l'art un prolongement de la religion, est celui d'un peintre de la Renaissance, et non celui de Musset. Mais cette conception dégage aussi le caractère sacré de la création artistique qui a pour but d'interpréter le monde, d'en livrer les secrets. En fin de compte, l'auteur de *Lorenzaccio* n'a-t-il pas, cachées au fond de lui, de semblables aspirations ? Ces vers du poème *Souvenir* (1841), dans lesquels il dédie à Dieu ses amours passées, expriment des sentiments assez proches de ceux de Tebaldeo :

« Je me dis seulement : A cette heure, en ce lieu,
Un jour, je fus aimé, j'aimais, elle était belle.
J'enfouis ce trésor dans mon âme immortelle,
Et je l'emporte à Dieu ».

L'art ne doit donc pas être galvaudé ; il doit être l'objet de toutes les dévotions, entouré d'un infini respect (Tebaldeo : « Je ne respecte point mon pinceau, mais je respecte mon art. Je ne puis faire le portrait d'une courtisane », Acte II, scène 2). L'artiste forme un tout. Il ne peut pas séparer sa vie quotidienne de son activité créatrice. Toutes ses actions, toute son existence doivent témoigner de son art. Honnêteté, indépendance, goût pour les occupations paisibles, telles sont les qualités de l'artiste, si l'on en juge par Tebaldeo (« Pourquoi m'en voudrait-on ? je ne fais de mal à personne (...). Personne ne me connaît, et je ne connais personne ; à qui ma vie ou ma mort peut-elle être utile ? », Acte II, scène 2).

62

L'art n'est donc pas coupé des réalités humaines : bien plus, il lui faut des circonstances particulières pour s'épanouir, des sources d'inspiration pour s'exalter. Tebaldeo développe une conception qui est tout à fait celle des romantiques. La création se satisfait des périodes troublées : la stabilité engendre des œuvres pures, mais faibles ; les chefs-d'œuvre ont besoin de grands bouleversements (« Il y a plusieurs cordes à la harpe des anges ; le zéphyr peut murmurer sur les faibles et tirer de leur accord une harmonie suave et délicieuse ; mais la corde d'argent ne s'ébranle qu'au passage du vent du nord », Acte II, scène 2). L'œuvre se nourrit de souffrance (« L'enthousiasme est frère de la souffrance », Acte II, scène 2).

C'est là une attitude qui semble proche de la position de Musset dont témoignent les fameux vers :
« Les plus désespérés sont les chants les plus beaux,
Et j'en sais d'immortels qui sont de purs sanglots[1] ».
Mais Lorenzaccio combat ironiquement cette sublimation de la douleur : « Je me ferais volontiers l'alchimiste de ton alambic ; les larmes des peuples y retombent en perles[2] » (Acte II, scène 2). Cette attaque de Lorenzo n'est-elle pas l'occasion pour Musset de rectifier une interprétation souvent tendancieuse donnée à cette conception des romantiques ? Toujours est-il qu'elle permet à Tebaldeo de préciser qu'il ne s'agit pas d'exploiter le « malheur des familles », mais d'établir une sympathie entre cette situation déplorable et l'art qui est lui-même souffrance (« Je dis que la poésie est la plus douce des souffrances, et qu'elle aime ses sœurs », Acte II, scène 2).

Inspiration et technique

L'art suppose une grande force d'imagination, car il se situe dans le domaine du rêve, et il faut être un puissant génie pour que se lève en soi l'inspiration indispensable à l'éclosion d'œuvres valables (Tebaldeo : « Réaliser des rêves, voilà la vie du peintre. Les plus grands ont représenté les leurs dans toute

---

1. *Nuit de mai* (1835).
2. Comme l'alambic de l'alchimiste qui transforme les substances, l'art, selon Tebaldeo, transformerait les larmes des peuples en perles.

leur force, et sans y rien changer. Leur imagination était un arbre plein de sève », Acte II, scène 2). Mais il n'est pas seulement la projection d'une inspiration. Il est aussi le résultat de longs efforts, l'aboutissement d'un long travail. Il donne lieu à une activité prenante, exige une discipline de vie nécessaire pour parvenir à des résultats satisfaisants. Il réclame un métier qui, seul, est capable d'amener l'artiste à choisir, de façon judicieuse, l'angle de vue à adopter ou la pose et le costume de son modèle.

Pour acquérir cette technique, une longue recherche est indispensable, enrichie par la méditation dans la solitude (« Je passe les journées à l'atelier », souligne Tebaldeo, Acte II, scène 2). Malgré les déceptions et les désillusions, il faut persévérer, ne pas reculer devant les difficultés (« Hélas ! les rêves des artistes médiocres sont des plantes difficiles à nourrir, et qu'on arrose de larmes bien amères pour les faire bien peu prospérer », Acte II, scène 2). Grâce à l'imitation et aux leçons des maîtres (« Seigneur, c'était mon maître », dit Tebaldeo de Raphaël, « Ce que j'ai appris vient de lui », Acte II, scène 2), de perfectionnement en perfectionnement, le talent s'affirmera.

Lorenzaccio et le mal du siècle romantique $\boxed{8}$

Tous ces thèmes profondément marqués par les apparences s'inscrivent eux-mêmes dans cette attitude désespérée des romantiques et de Musset devant la vie à laquelle on a donné le nom de mal du siècle. Celui-ci repose tout entier sur la conception d'un monde éclaté, divisé : le XVIIe siècle classique parvenait, tant bien que mal, à reconstituer l'unité de l'univers autour de valeurs idéales et figées ; le XVIIIe siècle y arrivait sans trop de difficultés, en prenant comme références la raison et le progrès ; les romantiques, au contraire, impuissants, constatent les contradictions irrémédiables dans lesquelles l'homme doit vivre.

LES TARES DE LA POLITIQUE ET DE LA SOCIÉTÉ

Incohérence de l'histoire

Le mal du siècle qu'éprouvent les romantiques est une attitude à laquelle on a souvent reproché son caractère artificiel, mais c'est également le résultat d'une réflexion provoquée par une situation politique dont ils sont amenés à prendre conscience. Depuis 1789, la France vit à l'heure des bouleversements. Les révolutions se succèdent. Les régimes remplacent les régimes. Tout système de références cohérent s'effondre, dans la multiplication des divergences, la ténuité des nuances. Aucune marche logique ne semble être suivie par l'histoire. Tout paraît être livré au hasard ou à des personnages providentiels qui surgissent et s'évanouissent tour à tour : Alexandre de Médicis assassiné, qu'importe ? Côme est là pour lui succéder. A l'époque de Musset, on espérait en Louis-Philippe. Il ne vaut pas mieux que Charles X. C'est de nouveau l'échec. Une fois de plus, les aspirations républicaines ont été trompées.

Dans *Lorenzaccio*, Musset n'a pas résisté à la tentation de juger les faits à travers son époque. L'évocation de l'Italie de la Renaissance doit beaucoup à la France contemporaine de l'auteur. L'insouciance du peuple et l'inconséquence des républicains qui ne savent pas exploiter la situation favorable, c'est la transposition de l'échec de 1830 qui a vu à une royauté, celle de Charles X, succéder une autre royauté, celle de Louis-Philippe, alors que tout était possible. L'attitude de Venturi et de Bindo qui acceptent les faveurs du duc (Acte II, scène 4), c'est le reflet de la compromission de certains républicains avec le pouvoir royal. La remarque du marchand : « C'est plaisir de voir ces bonnes dames, sortant de la messe, manier et examiner toutes les étoffes. Que Dieu conserve Son Altesse ! La cour est une belle chose » (Acte I, scène 2), c'est la transcription d'une mentalité, générale chez les commerçants de ces années 1830, qui soutenaient le régime du roi bourgeois, parce qu'il leur donnait toutes occasions de s'enrichir. La fin de la réplique de Philippe Strozzi : « Allons-y donc plus hardiment ! la république, il nous faut ce mot-là. Et quand ce ne serait qu'un mot, c'est quelque chose, puisque les peuples se lèvent quand il traverse l'air... » (Acte II, scène 1), c'est le cri des républicains avides de liberté.

Une société morcelée

Dans le domaine social, les fait parlent aussi et contribuent à créer l'arbitraire : une royauté acceptée par tous, parce que de droit divin, c'était la caution d'une hiérarchie qui ne reposait pas sur une disparité entre les différents individus, mais sur une décision irrévocable de la Providence, agissant dans le cadre de l'harmonie du monde ; une république, c'est la garantie de la liberté et de l'égalité dans le respect mutuel ; un régime de tendance monarchique suscité par les circonstances, qu'il soit imposé par des puissances étrangères, comme celui des Médicis, ou toléré avec plus ou moins de réticences, comme celui de Louis-Philippe, c'est une couverture com modément offerte à une minorité — les Salviati dans *Lorenzaccio* — pour opprimer la majorité.

Voilà qui contribue à morceler la société, à enfermer chaque groupe social à l'intérieur de ces barrières que représentent la naissance, l'argent, l'éducation, comme le souligne Lorenzo à propos de Gabrielle : « D'ailleurs, fille de bonnes gens (naissance), à qui leur peu de fortune (argent) n'a pas permis une éducation solide ; point de fond dans les principes, rien qu'un léger vernis » (Acte I, scène 1). Et ce cloisonnement est encore accentué par la montée des aspirations, des ambitions personnelles : elles aboutissent à l'aggravation des contradictions existant entre l'être individuel et l'être collectif, chacun ayant tendance, au lieu de contribuer au bonheur général, à exploiter le plus possible les avantages que lui offre une situation donnée : ainsi, le marchand, malgré son honnêteté, approuve la vie de fête de la cour, parce qu'il en profite pour s'enrichir (Acte I, scène 2).

LA FAILLITE DE L'HOMME

La réflexion sur l'essence, le rôle et le devenir de l'homme ne fait que confirmer ces leçons des événements. Le progrès aggrave, selon Musset, les inégalités sociales, parce qu'il aboutit à l'amélioration de l'existence des seuls privilégiés qui peuvent ainsi, grâce au travail des autres, se livrer à tous les plaisirs. Comment croire à la raison, devant le spectacle des soubresauts politiques, à la vue de l'inconséquence du peuple, qui, lorsque le gouverneur de la citadelle, le provéditeur Roberto Corsini, s'est offert « de livrer la forteresse aux amis de la liberté, avec les provisions, les clefs, et tout le reste (...) a braillé, bu du vin sucré, et cassé des carreaux » (Acte V, scène 5) ? La religion ? comment s'y fier, alors qu'elle a perdu son unité, qu'elle n'est plus un élément de référence absolue ?

L'action ? de quelque manière qu'on l'envisage, c'est un constat de faillite. Qu'elle engage la sensibilité, comme chez la marquise, c'est la trahison de soi-même ; qu'elle sollicite la réflexion, comme chez Philippe, c'est l'impuissance ; qu'elle fasse intervenir la détermination, comme chez Pierre, c'est l'aventure ; qu'elle se développe souterrainement, comme chez le cardinal, c'est la dissimulation, le machiavélisme ; qu'elle mette en œuvre enfin toutes les facultés, comme chez Lorenzaccio, c'est l'autodestruction. Dans tous les cas, c'est l'inutilité, la déception, l'échec : l'idéalisme réformateur aussi bien que l'activisme radical débouche sur le néant.

Les relations humaines ? Elles sont tout aussi décevantes : elles reposent sur l'ambiguïté, et sont à la merci de ces revirements qui font parfois subir à l'individu de monstrueuses métamorphoses. L'idéal ? Il est inaccessible, et crée l'orgueil et la démesure.

LE TRIOMPHE DU MAL

L'homme serait-il donc foncièrement mauvais ? Dans le jeu des contradictions qui le marquent, dans l'ambiguïté qui le caractérise, l'un des aspects l'emporte irrémédiablement. Et c'est malheureusement souvent celui qui satisfait ses mauvais instincts. La métamorphose qui s'opère en lui donne naissance à des monstres. C'est là une vision pessimiste qui repose sur cette conception débilitante selon laquelle les apparences sont en fait des masques d'honnêteté et de bonté bien fragiles, et que fatalement la vérité faite d'impureté et d'égoïsme arrivera à les arracher et à triompher.

Il ne suffit pour cela que de circonstances favorables. Et Lorenzaccio, qui, en émule d'Hamlet, a fait l'expérience de cette évolution hideuse et irréversible (« (...) je ne puis ni me retrouver moi-même ni laver mes mains, même avec du sang ! », constate-t-il à la scène 5 de l'Acte IV), éprouve un plaisir morbide à épier cette transformation monstrueuse : il la provoque chez Venturi et Bindo, en leur faisant accepter les faveurs ducales (Acte II, scène 4) ; il y contribue, en aidant à corrompre Gabrielle (« Voir dans une enfant de quinze ans la rouée à venir ; étudier, ensemencer, infiltrer paternellement le filon mystérieux du vice dans un conseil d'ami, dans une caresse au menton (...), habituer doucement l'imagination qui se développe à donner des corps à ses fantômes, à toucher ce qui l'effraie, à mépriser ce qui la protège ! », Acte I, scène 1) ; il la pressent chez Catherine (« J'allais corrompre Catherine », Acte IV, scène 5) ; il la juge universelle (« Je crois que je corromprais ma mère, si mon cerveau le prenait à tâche », Acte IV, scène 5).

A LA RECHERCHE DE RAISONS DE VIVRE

La croyance à un idéal

Comme ils ne peuvent supporter cette vision du monde, les écrivains romantiques tentent désespérément de la modifier, en faisant intervenir la notion bien commode d'espérance. Ils sont ainsi conduits à cautionner de tout leur être des activités dont ils parviennent tant bien que mal à estomper le sentiment d'inutilité qu'elles leur donnent, grâce à l'intensité de leur participation : ils se livrent résolument à l'action politique, comme Lamartine ou Hugo, pensant ainsi contribuer à la transformation de la société ; ils misent, comme Vigny, sur le triomphe à venir de la technique qui, changeant les données de la vie, changera par là même le comportement des individus ; ils substituent au culte de la raison le culte de la sensibilité, comme Musset ou Lamartine.

Le dépaysement

Si, en définitive, ces expédients apparaissent sous leur véritable jour, dans toute leur vanité, si décidément ils ne parviennent pas à se sentir bien, ni dans leur siècle, ni dans leur corps, ils essaieront de se bercer d'illusions, en utilisant des moyens d'évasion. Attirés par la nouveauté et le dépaysement, ils voyageront dans les pays étrangers, créateurs d'exotisme ; ce sera l'Orient pour Lamartine et Nerval, l'Italie pour Musset.

Se rendant compte que partout les problèmes se posent de façon identique, que rien ne change, ils feront appel à l'irréel ou au merveilleux, en tentant la plongée dans un autre univers, comme Hugo ou Nodier. Constatant que le mal est au fond d'eux-mêmes, ils s'efforceront de sortir de leur monde intérieur, d'échapper à leur vie monotone, en menant une existence théâtrale, en prenant des poses, en construisant un autre être, en se livrant à toutes ces excentricités dont Musset et Gautier ont donné tant d'exemples remarquables. Cet état d'esprit, qui explique, en partie, l'élaboration du personnage de Lorenzaccio, Musset l'exprimait déjà dans sa pièce précédente, en faisant dire à Fantasio : « Quelle admirable chose que *les Mille et une Nuits* ! O Spark ! mon cher Spark, si tu pouvais me transporter en Chine ! Si je pouvais seulement sortir de ma peau pendant une heure ou deux ! Si je pouvais être ce monsieur qui passe !» (Acte I, scène 2 de *Fantasio).*

Mais cette recherche débouche elle aussi sur l'impasse de l'échec. Tout se noie dans la mesquinerie. Même la nature a des imperfections, Fantasio le constate avec une ironie amère : « Comme ce soleil couchant est manqué ! La nature est pitoyable ce soir. Regarde-moi un peu cette vallée là-bas, ces quatre ou cinq méchants nuages qui grimpent sur cette montagne. Je faisais des paysages comme celui-là, quand j'avais douze ans, sur la couverture de mes livres de classe » (Acte I, scène 2).

Les « paradis artificiels »

Alors, il faut aider à l'évasion. Alors, il faut avoir recours à ces « paradis artificiels » que les romantiques cultiveront bien avant les symbolistes. Pour oublier le monde décevant, il faut se livrer au dérèglement des sens. Et tous les moyens sont bons : le vin, dont Musset abusait, et dont Lorenzaccio use lui aussi immodérément (« Peste soit de l'ivrogne et de ses farces silencieuses ! », dit de lui le provéditeur, Acte I, scène 2) ; la débauche, pratiquée par Musset comme par Lorenzaccio (« Mais j'aime le vin, le jeu et les filles », reconnaît-il, à la scène 3 de l'Acte III) ; la maladie, en partie conséquence de cette intempérance, qui n'a pas ménagé Musset, et qui n'épargne pas Lorenzaccio (« Regardez-moi ce petit corps maigre, ce lendemain d'orgie ambulant. Regardez-moi ces yeux plombés, ces mains fluettes et maladives, à peine assez fermes pour soutenir un éventail, ce visage morne, qui sourit quelquefois, mais qui n'a pas la force de rire », tel est le portrait peu flatteur que le duc fait de lui, à la scène 4 de l'Acte 1).

L'exaltation de la sensibilité

Ainsi pourra-t-on atteindre à cette exaltation de la sensibilité qui entraînait Musset dans des hallucinations, lui faisait voir « un pauvre enfant vêtu de noir », son double qui lui ressemblait « comme un frère[1] », et qui conduit Lorenzaccio au bord du délire, qui l'amène, dans la scène du meurtre simulé, à libérer son inconscient en un torrent de mots : « Meurs, infâme ! Je te saignerai, pourceau, je te saignerai ! Au cœur, au cœur ! il est éventré. — Crie donc, frappe donc, tue donc ! Ouvre-lui les entrailles ! Coupons-le par morceaux, et mangeons, mangeons ! J'en ai jusqu'au coude. Fouille dans la gorge, roule-le, roule ! Mordons, mordons, et mangeons ! », Acte III, scène 1).

Mais, contrairement à Musset, il manque à Lorenzaccio les deux divinités qui justifient la débauche de la sensibilité : l'amour et l'art.

---

1. *Nuit de décembre* (1835).

9

L'écriture théâtrale de *Lorenzaccio*

L'écriture d'une œuvre, c'est la « manière » de l'auteur, ce sont les techniques de rédaction utilisées pour mener à bien son élaboration, ce n'est pas seulement l'expression, mais plus globalement le parti pris stylistique retenu, par exemple la position adoptée dans le choix des tonalités — comique, dramatique, tragique, etc. — dans la conduite des récits, des descriptions, de la peinture des caractères. L'écriture théâtrale, c'est tout l'art de tenir compte des conditions particulières du genre, de donner la vie aux personnages, de rendre naturels les dialogues. Ce qui frappe dans *Lorenzaccio*, c'est la variété de cette écriture, c'est la diversité introduite aussi bien dans les formes que dans les registres.

LA VARIÉTÉ DES FORMES

La diversité des formes est étonnante. Elle apparaît d'abord dans la nature même des répliques. Parfois, Musset procède par interventions rapides (Acte I, scène 2), utilise une expression volontairement négligée propre à la langue parlée (début de la scène 3 de l'Acte III), accumule les exclamations qui animent le style (Acte II, scène 5), multiplie les interrogations qui relancent le dialogue (Acte I, scène 1).

Mais il sacrifie aussi aux tirades interminables, à ces véritables dissertations en style soutenu, à ces morceaux de bravoure hérités de la tradition classique et cultivés de façon si excessive par tous les dramaturges romantiques : les développements successifs auxquels se livre Lorenzaccio, à la scène 3 de l'Acte IV, sont, à cet égard, significatifs.

Il ménage de savants contrastes entre les grands mouvements de foule (Acte I, scène 2) et les moments d'intimité (Acte I, scène 3). Il fait se succéder peintures des caractères (voir le portrait que fait la marquise du cardinal à la scène 3 de l'Acte II), parties descriptives (voir l'évocation champêtre de

Lorenzo à la scène 9 de l'Acte IV) et récits (voir le résumé que fait Lorenzo de son action à la scène 3 de l'Acte III).

LE MÉLANGE DES REGISTRES

Les registres utilisés par Musset sont eux aussi des plus variés. Le mélange des genres est total. Le comique de farce apparaît, par exemple, dans l'opposition entre la politesse pédante des précepteurs et la hargne du petit Salviati et du petit Strozzi (Acte V, scène 5). Un comique plus léger, fait d'humour, naît de la description de l'air affairé et important des écoliers qui contemplent de loin la fête chez les Nasi (Acte I, scène 2). La vulgarité de la conduite de l'officier, lors de l'arrestation des Strozzi, contraste avec la haute tenue des propos de Lorenzaccio lorsqu'il fait part à Philippe de sa conception de l'existence (Acte III, scène 3). Le mélodrame se déchaîne dans la mise en scène de l'empoisonnement de Louise et de l'égarement de son père (Acte III, scène 7). Le tragique pèse de tout son poids, avec la mort de Lorenzo qui n'aura « pas même un tombeau » (Acte V, scène 6).

Parmi ces registres variés, le lyrisme, cette exaltation des sentiments chère aux poètes, occupe une place importante. Dans *Lorenzaccio*, Musset exprime tout son sens poétique. Il utilise une langue riche, séduisante, pleine d'images somptueuses. Tantôt, c'est l'évocation simple et familière d'une nature apaisante, comme dans la description que fait Catherine à la scène 6 de l'Acte I : « Le soleil commence à baisser. De larges bandes de pourpre traversent le feuillage, et la grenouille fait sonner sous les roseaux sa petite cloche de cristal ». Tantôt, c'est la comparaison frappante, suggestive, comme celle de Lorenzo qui s'assimile aux « masques de plâtre » (Acte III, scène 3). Tantôt, c'est la métaphore longuement développée, comme lorsque l'orfèvre décrit les transformations de Florence par « deux architectes malavisés », le pape et l'empereur (Acte I, scène 2). Toujours, c'est la recherche du mot juste, le recours à des données concrètes, puisées dans la vie quotidienne, mais sublimées par le souffle de l'inspiration, pour illustrer l'idée, pour la rendre plus sensible, pour mieux l'exprimer.

10

Les interprétations de *Lorenzaccio*

Jusqu'au premier tiers du XXe siècle, les critiques se montrent réticents dans les jugements qu'ils portent sur *Lorenzaccio*. Il s'agit là en fait d'une attitude générale envers l'ensemble du théâtre de Musset. Ce qu'on apprécie alors en lui, c'est le poète, l'auteur des *Nuits*. Quant à son talent de dramaturge, il est mis en doute. Son écriture théâtrale est rarement approuvée. On l'accuse volontiers d'invraisemblances. On considère que c'est pour la lecture qu'il a conçu son théâtre, qu'on a donc tendance à juger sur ses vertus littéraires plus que sur sa valeur dramaturgique.

Aucune représentation de *Lorenzaccio* ne se déroule d'ailleurs du vivant de son auteur. Les raisons politiques — la pièce était considérée comme subversive — expliquent autant que les difficultés techniques une telle mise à l'écart. La création n'a lieu qu'en 1896 au Théâtre de la Renaissance à Paris. Il s'agit en fait d'une version très remaniée due à Armand d'Artois. La grande Sarah Bernhardt assure la mise en scène et interprète le personnage de Lorenzaccio. Dans un décor réaliste, elle insiste plutôt sur la signification psychologique et « gomme » la dimension politique. Vêtue de noir, elle joue, comme à son habitude, sur les attitudes et sur les expressions du visage : « (...) dès la première scène », souligne Félix Duquesnel dans son compte rendu, « l'effet est saisissant, cet être pâle, maladif, ce corps d'éphèbe à demi courbé (...), tout cela est d'une vérité terrifiante ».

La tradition de confier le rôle de Lorenzaccio à une femme est désormais établie et a pour effet de renforcer le caractère efféminé du personnage. Elle marque, en particulier, l'entrée de l'œuvre à la Comédie-Française en 1927. Dans une adaptation et une mise en scène d'Émile Fabre qui affiche un souci de reconstitution historique, le rôle principal est interprété par Marie-Thérèse Piérat.

A partir des années trente, la vision évoluera progressivement. Musset prendra un autre visage. Ce que l'on va maintenant louer en lui, plus ou moins au détriment de son œuvre poétique, c'est justement ce qui lui était refusé, le génie dramatique. Il apparaîtra comme le grand dramaturge du XIXe siècle : ses pièces, en particulier *Lorenzaccio*, seront posées comme les seules réussites théâtrales du romantisme.

Les mises en scène se diversifient. L'on tend à revenir à la version originale de la pièce, mais la tentation de couper et de modifier un texte dense et difficile à monter demeure. En 1945, Gaston Baty insiste, à son tour, sur l'aspect somptueux et grandiose de Florence où évolue un Lorenzaccio incarné par Marguerite Jamois.

En 1952, c'est le grand tournant dans l'histoire de la pièce. C'est enfin un comédien qui se charge du personnage de Lorenzaccio. Gérard Philipe joue le rôle et, conseillé par Jean Vilar, assure la mise en scène. Les représentations ont lieu en plein air, lors du festival d'Avignon, ce qui permet de rendre avec bonheur ces mouvements de foule si importants dans le déroulement de l'action. Vêtu d'un pourpoint noir agrémenté de flammes rouges, Gérard Philipe excelle à dégager l'ambiguïté du personnage à la fois faible et héroïque, perverti et attiré par un idéal inaccessible. Il insiste également sur la signification politique de la pièce qui apparaît comme la tragédie de la mort de la liberté.

Plus près de nous, en 1969, Guy Rétoré souligne, à son tour, la dimension politique : pour lui, Musset a voulu, à la fois, représenter la situation de son époque et poser le problème général de la tyrannie. Le caractère symbolique du décor est là pour le suggérer, tandis que Gérard Désarte incarne un Lorenzo, symbole universel de l'engagement.

En 1976, dans la mise en scène de Franco Zeffirelli, Florence occupe une place centrale, est un véritable personnage. Francis Huster interprète un Lorenzaccio complexe, terrifiant et pur, poussé par trois impulsions : son amour pour le duc, sa conception politique et son obsession de la mort.

Bibliographie

Les éditions

Parmi les nombreuses éditions de l'œuvre de Musset, signalons plus particulièrement les deux intégrales :
- Alfred de Musset, *Œuvres complètes*, Paris, Cercle du bibliophile, 1969, en 10 volumes. En plus des œuvres de Musset au texte soigneusement établi (*Lorenzaccio* figure dans le tome IV), on trouvera une bibliographie, une chronologie et des notes abondantes de Gilbert Sigaux, les notes biographiques rédigées par Paul de Musset ainsi qu'une élégante illustration de Bida.
- Alfred de Musset, Œuvres complètes, édition Philippe Van Tieghem, Paris, Éditions du Seuil, collection « L'Intégrale », 1963. Édition pratique qui réunit toute l'œuvre de Musset en un seul volume.

Pour le théâtre complet, on conseillera :
- Alfred de Musset, *Théâtre complet*, Paris, le Livre de Poche, 1964-1965 ; en trois volumes (*Lorenzaccio* se trouve au tome I). Une préface de René Clair donne une interprétation originale du théâtre de Musset ; une introduction et des notes succinctes, mais précises, d'Yves Florenne éclairent les points les plus délicats.

Le romantisme

Pour une approche du romantisme, lire l'ouvrage de :
- Louis-Verdun Saulnier, *la Littérature française du Siècle romantique*, Paris, Éditions des PUF, collection « Que sais-je ? », 1969, étude qui donne le point de l'état actuel des recherches sur la littérature du XIXe siècle.

Sur le théâtre romantique, outre l'ouvrage précédent, on pourra consulter avec profit :
- Maurice Descotes, *le Drame romantique et ses Grands Créateurs*, Paris, Éditions des PUF, 1954, qui fournit de précieuses indications sur les conditions de création et de représentation des pièces marquantes du romantisme.

La vie et l'œuvre de Musset

Deux titres à conseiller :
- Léon Lafoscade, *le Théâtre d'Alfred de Musset*, Paris, Éditions Nizet, 1966, étude d'ensemble de l'œuvre théâtrale.
- Philippe Soupault, *Alfred de Musset*, Paris, Éditions Seghers, collection « Poètes d'aujourd'hui », 1966, qui contient un choix intéressant de textes.

Études sur *Lorenzaccio*

- Éric L. Gans, *Musset et le Drame tragique*, Paris, Éditions José Corti, 1974, où se trouve notamment soulignée toute la dimension tragique de *Lorenzaccio*.

- André Lebois, *Vues sur le Théâtre de Musset*, Avignon, Éditions Aubanel, 1966, dont le chapitre 1, consacré à *Une analyse spectrale de* Lorenzaccio, fouille la pièce jusque dans ses moindres recoins.

- Henri Lefebvre, *Alfred de Musset dramaturge*, Paris, Éditions de l'Arche, 1955, dont le chapitre 4 fournit des documents précieux sur la mise en scène et les représentations de la pièce.

- Bernard Masson, *Musset et son Double : lecture de Lorenzaccio*, Paris, Éditions Minard, 1978, qui contient, à côté d'une interprétation moderne de l'œuvre, des indications intéressantes sur les conditions de sa rédaction.

- Maurice Toesca, *Alfred de Musset ou l'Amour de la Mort*, Paris, Éditions Hachette, 1970, qui analyse un des thèmes essentiels de *Lorenzaccio*.

Index des thèmes

Références aux pages « Profil »	Références à Lorenzaccio (actes et scènes)
Mouvements de foule, 13, 18, 19, 23, 27, 30, 33, 34, 35, 78, 79, 55, 72.	I,2 ; I, 5 ; III, 3 ; IV, 2 ; V, 3 ; V, 4 ; V, 5 ; V, 7 ;
Peinture des caractères, 9, 10, 46, 50, 55, 64, 65, 71	I, 1 ; I, 3 ; I, 4 ; II, I ; II, 2 ; II, 3 ; II, 5 ; II, 6 ; III, 2 ; III, 3 ; III, 6 ; IV, 3 ; IV, 9 ; V, 1.
Philosophie, 7, 8, 9, 12, 13, 23, 24, 46, 51, 52, 53, 60, 61, 62, 63, 67, 68	I, 2 ; II, 3 ; III, 3 ; IV, 3.
Poésie/lyrisme, 56, 72, 73.	I, 3 ; IV, 1 ; IV, 3 ; IV, 9.
Pouvoir, 11, 12, 19, 20, 25, 28, 29, 30, 31, 32, 33, 34, 49, 50, 65, 66.	I, 2 ; I, 4 ; II, 1 ; II, 5 ; III, 6 ; IV, 4 ; V, 1 ; V, 7.
Pureté, 13, 18, 23, 24, 26, 30, 47, 48, 50, 58, 59, 60, 61.	I, 1 ; I, 6 ; II, 4 ; IV, 3 ; IV, 5 ; IV, 9.
Religion, 21, 26, 28, 52, 54, 66.	I, 3 ; II, 2 ; III, 6.
Romantisme, 6, 7, 8, 9, 10, 12, 13, 14, 72, 73.	I, I ; I, 6 ; II, 2 ; II, 4 ; III, 3 ; III, 6 ; IV, 3 ; IV, 9.
Théâtralité, 14, 15, 16, 17, 18, 30, 31, 72, 73	I, 2 ; I, 3 ; I, 5 ; II, 6 ; II, 7 ; III, I ; III, 7 ; IV, 6 ; V, 5.

Aubin Imprimeur
LIGUGÉ, POITIERS

Achevé d'imprimer en janvier 1992
No d'édition 8715 / No d'impression L 39217
Dépôt légal janvier 1992 / Imprimé en France

Contents

Introducing Bangkok

The energy of Bangkok is intoxicating, and visitors, whether they stay just a couple of days to see the main sights or spend longer and look a little deeper, come away with lasting impressions of a city that lives life in the fast lane.

The view from the road or train into the city is of futuristic high-rises and multilane highways, but at street level the contrasts are stark. The many street markets buzz with activity as residents bargain hard for food and necessities, but nearby well-heeled shoppers head into glitzy shopping malls packed with designer brands. In the early morning the monks, eyes down and clutching their traditional bowls, walk silently in line along the streets collecting alms from the locals; just behind them bleary-eyed bar girls and revelers make their way home.

The evening crowds meander along the narrow streets taking their time in choosing what to eat from one of the many street food stands, where the food is freshly cooked; nearby the choice of restaurants is legendary, ranging from places selling simple traditional dishes to those with white tablecloths, gleaming cutlery and rooftops with views to die for.

The end of the 20th century saw an extraordinary building boom here—with a subsequent increase in traffic. The Skytrain and Metro system relieve the pressure and these transportation lines continue to be extended, opening up new parts of the city to be explored. The constant movement of boats on the Chao Phraya River is relentless, but a river boat is still a fun and efficient way of getting around, particularly in the Rattanakosin area.

Since 2014, Thailand has been under military government, but the impact on visitors has been minimal. In fact, in 2017 Bangkok was the world's most visited city, with 20 million international arrivals. Wherever you go and whatever you do, join in the all-pervasive *sanuk* (fun) and any language barriers will melt away.

FACTS AND FIGURES

- 9.45 million residents
- 95 percent of Bangkokians are Buddhists
- Bangkok's full ceremonial name runs to 169 characters—Krung Thep Mahanakhon Amon Rattanakosin Mahinthara Ayuthaya Mahadilok Phop Noppharat Ratchathani Burirom Udomratchaniwet Mahasathan Amon Piman Awatan Sathit Sakkathattiya Witsanukam Prasit.

SABAI SABAI

For Thais, happiness is closely linked to tranquility and while the word *sabai* is often translated as "happy," its true meaning is closer to "relaxed" or "comfortable." It's a sense of wellness. One way Thais emphasize an adjective is to simply repeat it. Think of "not a care in the world" and you have a fairly accurate English translation of *sabai sabai*.

LONG LIVE THE KING

The national anthem is played at Hua Lamphong Station, before movies and on television at 8am and 6pm daily. H.M. King Bhumibol Adulyadej (Rama IX), the world's longest reigning monarch, passed away in October 2016 and was succeeded by his son, Maha Vajiralongkorn, Rama X. The official coronation ceremony is expected to be in 2019.

THE NEW CAPITAL

In 1768, after the Burmese destroyed Ayutthaya, General Phraya Taksin established a new capital at Thonburi, where he was crowned King Boromaraja IV (known as King Taksin). In 1782, Taksin was deposed by a general, who became Rama I. His new capital was Krung Thep (City of Angels); today the city is known as Bangkok.

A Short Stay in Bangkok

DAY 1

Morning Start early, before it gets steamy, with a visit to Wat Phra Kaew and the **Grand Palace** (▷ 24–25), two superb examples of Thai art and architecture, which cannot be missed. Stroll over to the temple compound of **Wat Pho** (▷ 34–35), to admire the huge reclining Buddha, the carvings of the *Ramakien*, and then finish off the visit with an authentic Thai massage on the grounds.

Lunch There are few lunch options in this area, so walk across the green oasis of **Sanam Luang** (▷ 40–41) and then hop on a ferry from Tha Tien pier to Tha Phra Athit for some tasty vegetarian food at **May Kaidee's** (▷ 46).

Afternoon After lunch walk around Banglamphu and Thanon Khao San and shop for some inexpensive souvenirs.

Mid-afternoon Around 3pm arrange a long-tail boat to take you from Tha Phra Athit pier along the scenic **Khlong Bangkok Yai** canal (▷ 100–101) to Thonburi, with a stop at the dazzling Temple of the Dawn, **Wat Arun** (▷ 32).

Dinner Go for cocktails on the immensely high roof terrace of **Moon Bar** (▷ 65), and then take a taxi to **Eat Me** (▷ 67) for some delightful fusion food and great atmosphere.

Evening After a long day, grab a taxi and meander through the Pak Khlong Talat flower market (▷ 28) where the heavily scented night air is intoxicating.

DAY 2

Morning Have a leisurely breakfast on the beautiful terrace of the Mandarin Oriental Hotel (▷ 58, 112), watching the busy traffic on the Chao Phraya River. Stroll over to the delightful **Museum for Bangkokians** (▷ 58–59) with its peaceful garden and interesting mix of Thai, Chinese, Indian and European elements (call ahead for a guided tour by the lady who grew up there). For a very different and definitely more glamorous approach to Thai architecture, take a taxi, or Skytrain, to **Baan Jim Thompson** (▷ 72–73) near Siam Square, with one of the world's best collections of traditional Thai paintings.

Lunch After a visit to the elegant and fascinating house on the *khlong*, have lunch at the stylish bar and restaurant in Jim Thompson's House.

Afternoon It is a short walk from the house to Siam Square, where you can spend the afternoon shopping at the **Siam Paragon** shopping mall (▷ 86), **Narai Phand** emporium (▷ 85) and **Emporium** (▷ 84). If you prefer more architecture to shopping, head for the Dusit area and visit the stunning royal **Phra Thi Nang Vimanmek** (▷ 75) or take a guided cycling tour (▷ 119) and explore beyond the main drag. Relax before dinner with a good massage at one of the city's many spas; **Banyan Tree Spa** (▷ 64) is particularly recommended.

Dinner Head for one of the fashionable eateries off Sukhumvit Road, such as **Chi Ultralounge** (▷ 88) or **Basil** (▷ 90).

Evening Finish the night in one of the city's many clubs (▷ 44, 88, 89), or try out one of the great jazz cafés like **The Living Room** (▷ 89).

Top 25

► ► ►

ESSENTIAL BANGKOK TOP 25

8

These pages are a quick guide to the Top 25, which are described in more detail later. Here they are listed alphabetically, and the tinted background shows which area they are in.

Chatuchak Weekend Market ▷ 98 Bangkok's largest market has thousands of stands.

Chinatown ▷ 50 It's all about buying and selling in this teeming mayhem of streets and alleys.

Grand Palace ▷ 24 One-time home of the Thai royal family, this complex should not be missed.

Khlong Bangkok Yai ▷ 100 A river cruise is a most welcome escape from the city's traffic chaos.

M.R. Kukrit Heritage House ▷ 52 Traditional teak house, home to a former prime minister.

Mae Nam Chao Phraya ▷ 26 See the grand buildings along the banks of Bangkok's river.

Pak Khlong Talat ▷ 28 Thailand's largest flower market is a riot of exotic color.

Phra Thi Nang Vimanmek ▷ 75 The world's largest golden teak mansion is a haven of tranquility.

Pipitaphan (National Museum) ▷ 29 A dimly lit treasure trove.

Prasart Museum ▷ 102 Thai antiquities in beautiful, traditional houses.

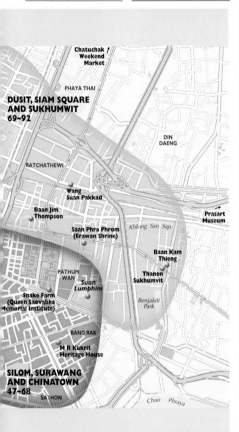

Snake Farm ▷ 54 Fascinating research center where you can get up close to snakes.

Saan Phra Phrom ▷ 76 The Erawan Shrine in the midst of designer stores is said to bring good fortune.

Royal Barges Museum ▷ 30 Splendid carved barges—the Rolls Royces of the waterways.

◀ ◀ ◀

Shopping

With several megamalls to choose from, as well as weekend and night markets, you can shop round the clock. Handwoven silks, traditional crafts, designer wear and trendy Oriental design or spa products offer almost endless choice. Shopping in Bangkok is exhilarating but can be utterly exhausting, and then there is the headache of whether you can cram it all in your baggage allowance on the plane.

Bargain Buys

It's hard to resist bargains. Traditional markets are bursting with exotic produce and well-made handicrafts. Ultrasmart shopping malls stock the latest from Prada or Louis Vuitton (albeit only in tiny Asian sizes) as well as new local designers. If you don't find the clothes, shoes or furniture you want, you can have it made within a few days. Fabrics are a good buy. Thai silk comes in several weights and a variety of rich and subtle colors and patterns. H.M. Queen Sirikit has made great efforts to promote Mudmee, the hand-woven silk produced in Northeastern Thailand. The Phahurat area is lined with shops selling Indian silks and synthetics, batiks and traditional Thai cotton clothing are sold at the Chatuchak Weekend Market (▷ 98–99).

Traditional Items

Good crafts, locally made or imported from neighboring Laos, Cambodia or Myanmar, come in a great selection at specialist shops

Buy from street markets and elegant malls

SHOP TILL YOU DROP

Siam Paragon shopping mall (▷ 86) has Western designer labels and Thai design and crafts. Several young Thai designers have stores on Siam Square, a teenage heaven for wacky jewelry and accessories. Sukhumvit Road is the place to go for good tailors and Thai silk products, but also has stalls selling fake designer brands and DVDs. Khao San Road is good for inexpensive clothes, CDs and jewelry. The best all-round place for crafts, clothes and antiques is the Chatuchak Weekend Market (▷ 98–99).

and markets. The inexpensive triangular pillows (*mawn khaan*) make great gifts, although they are heavy and bulky to carry back. Benjarong, traditional royal Thai porcelain, is covered in brightly glazed enamel and used as food containers or serving dishes. You can buy simple but fine celadon, glazed pottery that comes in jade green, purple, blue and brown. Nielloware, silver objects inlaid with niello, and bronze and hand-beaten brassware are other good buys.

Authentic Antiques
Although fine antiques from all over the region are available in Bangkok, don't expect bargains. The best and priciest objects can be found at the River City Shopping Complex (▷ 63); less expensive goods at the Chatuchak Weekend Market (▷ 98–99). Reputable shops will help you get the necessary export permit for most antiques. Otherwise you must apply for a license from the Fine Arts Department at the Ministry of Culture (tel 0 2221 7811).

Jewels Galore
Jewelry and cut or uncut gems, particularly blue sapphires and rubies, are excellent value. You need to know what you are buying— sometimes tinted glass is passed off as gems. Reputable jewelers belong to "The Jewel Fest Club" and will issue a certificate of authenticity and a guarantee to refund (less 10 percent) if goods are returned within 30 days. Pay with a credit card for added protection.

Clothes, fabrics and antiques are good buys

SPA DELIGHTS

With the booming spa culture comes a large range of spa products made in Thailand with Oriental spices and perfumes. The products are good quality, wonderful value and make nice presents. The better-known brands are THANN, HARRN and the chic Pañpuri. The THANN Sanctuary in Bangkok was chosen as one of the best spas in the world. All of these brands have shops in the Emporium and Siam Paragon as well as in other shopping malls in the city, and at Suvarnabhumi airport.

Shopping by Theme

Whether you're looking for a mall, a department store, a quirky boutique or something in between, you'll find it all in Bangkok. On this page shops are listed by theme. For a more detailed write-up, see the individual listings in Bangkok by Area.

Books/Prints
Asia Books ▷ 61
Kinokuniya ▷ 85
Shaman Books ▷ 43

Clothes
Greyhound ▷ 84
Herrmann Fashions ▷ 84
Narry Tailor ▷ 85
Tailor on Ten ▷ 86
Universal Tailors ▷ 63

Crafts
Exothique Thai ▷ 84
Good Shepherd ▷ 84
Lin Silvercraft ▷ 62
Lofty Bamboo ▷ 43
Narai Phand ▷ 85

Department Store
Robinson ▷ 86

Food
Nittaya Curry Shop ▷ 43

Household
L'Arcadia ▷ 84
Elephant House ▷ 43
Loft ▷ 62

Papaya ▷ 85
Pirun Thong ▷ 86
Propaganda ▷ 86
Siam Bronze Factory
    ▷ 63
Thai Home Industries
    ▷ 63

Jewelry
Bangkok Fashion Outlet
    ▷ 61
Johny's Gems ▷ 62
Lambert Industries Ltd
    ▷ 62

Malls
Asiatique Riverfront ▷ 61
Emporium Shopping
    Complex ▷ 84
Gaysorn Plaza ▷ 84
Mahboonkrong (MBK)
    Center ▷ 85
Old Siam Plaza ▷ 62
Pantip Plaza ▷ 85
River City Shopping
    Complex ▷ 63
Siam Paragon ▷ 86
Silom Village ▷ 63

Markets
Amulet Market ▷ 43
Patpong Night Bazaar
    ▷ 62
Sampeng Lane Market
    ▷ 63
Thanon Khao San Market
    ▷ 43

Miscellaneous
Hej Street Beauty ▷ 61
Knot ▷ 85
Refill Station ▷ 86

Textiles
Almeta ▷ 84
Anita Thai Silk ▷ 61
The Fine Arts ▷ 61
H.M. Factory for Thai Silk
    ▷ 84
Jim Thompson's Thai Silk
    Company ▷ 62
Prayer Textile Gallery
    ▷ 86
Taekee Taekon ▷ 43

Thai Art
H Gallery ▷ 61

Bangkok by Night

Thais have a much-used word, *sanuk* (meaning fun, pleasure), and they love to enjoy themselves. The authorities tend to impose "curfews" in a somewhat random manner, but most night spots are open until around 2am.

Bars and Nightclubs

From roadside watering holes to cocktail bars in garden settings and seriously chic rooftop lounges, Bangkok really does cater to everyone. Silom Road is mainly popular with local workers and expats but has some excellent spots for drinks and dinner. The *soi* (lanes) off Sukhumvit Road are home to many smart bars, restaurants and upscale hotel cocktail lounges. The areas of Nana Plaza and Soi Cowboy are red-light districts and can be rather sleazy.

An Evening Stroll

Walk through Patpong (▷ 59) and Silom Road's night market. Watch out for the cheap fakes, from Rolexes, T-shirts and DVDs to the latest PlayStation games and Vuitton suitcases. Khao San and Banglamphu also make for a good evening stroll.

Romantic Bangkok

For a romantic alfresco meal take a dinner cruise on the Chao Phraya River (▷ 26) and see the floodlit Grand Palace and Wat Arun, or have dinner on the terrace of one of the five-star hotels overlooking the river.

Bangkok's nightlife has plenty to offer

WHAT'S ON

Bangkok's excellent English-language daily newspapers—*Bangkok Post* and *The Nation*—have listings of all cultural events as well as news and reviews of new restaurants, venues and attractions. The monthly *Bangkok 101* magazine, available from bookshops, is good for listings as well as notices about new bars, restaurants or shops. Several free listings magazines, including *Where*, *Big Chilli* and *BK Magazine*, can be found in trendy bars and restaurants. Tickets can be booked at thaiticketmaster.com.

Where to Eat

Eating is one of the great pleasures in Bangkok. Thais eat out several times a day. Thai food is delicious once you get used to the exuberant use of chilies. Restaurants cater to every budget, and the range of foods is fantastic: from a great spicy seafood curry at a roadside stall to black cod at a trendy Sukhumvit eatery.

Thai Cuisine

Thai food is a mixture of indigenous cooking fused with some Chinese and Indian styles. It can be chili-fueled or bland depending on the region where it originated. It typically uses lemongrass and galangal, which give that special Thai taste. Coconut thickens the sauce and adds its own richness, while lime leaves, fresh cilantro (coriander) leaves, Thai basil and whole fresh peppercorns usually end up in there, too. A milder option is authentic Chinese restaurants—or the stalls in Chinatown (▷ 50).

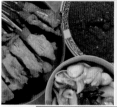

Where to Eat

The areas with the greatest concentration of quality restaurants with menus in English are to be found around Thanon Sukhumvit and Thanon Silom. Many of the best restaurants, especially ones serving non-Thai cuisine, are in good hotels, while the best-value places to eat are food courts and at street stands. In and around Thanon Khao San in Banglamphu there are also inexpensive places to enjoy good food. If you are shopping in one of the big malls, try their popular food courts, usually located in the basement.

THE LOVE OF FOOD

Thais love eating, as is obvious from the wide selection of restaurants in Bangkok—it is claimed that there are more than 50,000, and that's not counting the foodstalls that set up on every street and the food boats along the canals. You won't go hungry, that's for sure. But if your heart is set on one particular restaurant, be sure to make a reservation—others might feel the same way about it.

Enjoy Thai cuisine in sleek restaurants and street cafés

Where to Eat by Cuisine

There are plenty of places to eat to suit all tastes and budgets in Bangkok. On this page they are listed by cuisine. For a more detailed description of each venue, see Bangkok by Area.

Top Tips For...

These great suggestions will help you tailor your ideal visit to Bangkok, no matter how you choose to spend your time. Each sight or listing has a fuller write-up elsewhere in the book.

A LAZY MORNING
Have a leisurely breakfast on the terrace of the Mandarin Oriental Hotel, watching the activity on the river as the express boats dash up and down taking Bangkokians to work (▷ 58).
Go for an early morning stroll in Lumphini Park (▷ 55) and watch masses of Thais do their daily t'ai chi routines.
Take a long-tail boat on Khlong Bangkok Yai (▷ 100–101) to escape the city noise.

PAMPERING
Spend the day or the weekend being pampered at The Oriental Spa (▷ 58) or Banyan Tree Spa (▷ 64).
Make a traditional massage part of your visit to Wat Pho (▷ 44), home of Thailand's main training school for traditional treatments.
If your feet are weary from all the sightseeing, head to one of the many side-street spas in the Sukhumvit and Silom Road areas for a wonderful one-hour reflexology massage (▷ 89).

SHOPPING SPREES
The Chatuchak Weekend Market (▷ 98–99) has more than you can bargain for, and is now easily reached by Skytrain and Metro.
The Siam Paragon (▷ 86) is one of the city's most glamorous shopping malls, with a huge cinema complex and food court.
The Emporium Shopping Complex (▷ 84) and the neighboring Emquartier have top designer stores on the lower levels and more mid-range choices higher up, along with myriad food outlets, a cinema and roller dome.
Throw yourself into the melée that is Sampeng Lane market (▷ 63) in Chinatown, but sharpen your bargaining skills first.

Clockwise from top left: Long-tail boat on Khlong Bangkok Yai; kites in Sanam Luang park; Wat Phra Kaew; floating

CULTURE TRAILS

See one of the few houses in the city to survive World War II at the Museum for Bangkokians (▷ 58–59), and understand more about the people of Bangkok.

Take a walk in old Rattanakosin (▷ 42), passing the spectacular Grand Palace, a number of wats and street markets, and crossing over a canal and Sanam Luang.

Head for the quiet of M.R. Kukrit Heritage House (▷ 52–53), with its historic teak houses set in peaceful gardens.

TEMPLES

It's a must to go to see Wat Phra Kaew (▷ 25) in the Grand Palace complex, home to the very sacred Emerald Buddha.

Low-key Wat Traimit (▷ 56–57) houses the largest solid gold Buddha in the world.

See the sun set over Wat Arun (▷ 32–33) from one of the many rooftop bars across the river.

GREEN SPACES

Practice t'ai chi in Lumphini Park (▷ 55), join in a late-afternoon aerobics session, or simply go for a stroll or row a boat on the lake.

Admire the kite-flying skills as exotic shapes swoop overhead at Sanam Luang (▷ 40–41) and teams with fighting kites show off.

Cycle on the narrow pathways along the Thonburi *khlongs* (▷ 100–101) through villages with stilt houses set in gardens.

BUDGET ROOMS

Furama Xclusive Sukhumvit (▷ 109), in the heart of the Sukhumvit shopping and nightlife district, is a perfect choice for those who want a boutique hotel without the designer price tag.

The Atlanta (▷ 109), a place where you step back in time, has achieved legendary status among the city's inexpensive sleeps.

Wake up to the gentle lapping of the river and soft put-put of long-tailed boats at the River View Guest House (▷ 109).

kitchen in Thonburi; typical street in Chinatown; roses for sale at Chatuchak Weekend Market; relaxing Thai spa

CHILDREN'S ACTIVITIES

Kids love speeding along the river and into the canals on the brightly decorated long-tail boats (▷ 100, 118).

Young children will love the animals, feeding times and entertainments on offer at Safari World (▷ 103).

Pass a few hours at the interactive Children's Discovery Museum (▷ 103), with lots of fun activities including an adventure playground, water park and cultural program.

On a rainy day there is no better place than SEA LIFE Bangkok Ocean World (▷ 82) to investigate all things marine, including sharks, colorful jellyfish and gentoo penguins.

BEING THRIFTY

It's not entirely free, but very inexpensive, to hop on a river ferry just before sunset when Bangkok looks ageless and beautiful.

Night owls can admire the rows and rows of fragrant, colorful flowers at Pak Khlong Talat flower market (▷ 28), which is at its best after dark.

Watch the crowds make offerings at the Erawan Shrine (▷ 76–77) and pay for traditional Thai dancers.

GREAT VIEWS

Sip a cocktail on one of the world's highest roof terraces, the Banyan Tree Hotel's Moon Bar (▷ 65).

Take a room at the Peninsula hotel (▷ 112), or eat at its riverside restaurant, and see the city in all its glory.

View the grandeur of the royal city of Rattanakosin from up high on one of the glorious golden *chedi* on the Golden Mount near Wat Saket (▷ 39).

ALTERNATIVE BANGKOK

Chang Chui Creative Park (▷ 96–97), a one-stop cultural melting pot with street performers, artisans, theaters and food stalls, is Bangkok's most popular new creation.

From top: A long-tail boat on the canals; Erawan Shrine; The Peninsula Hotel and Terrace; view from Wat Saket

Bangkok by Area

and Around

Rattanakosin is the sacred heart of Bangkok, with some of the country's holiest monuments, as well as the former royal residence, the Grand Palace.

Top 25

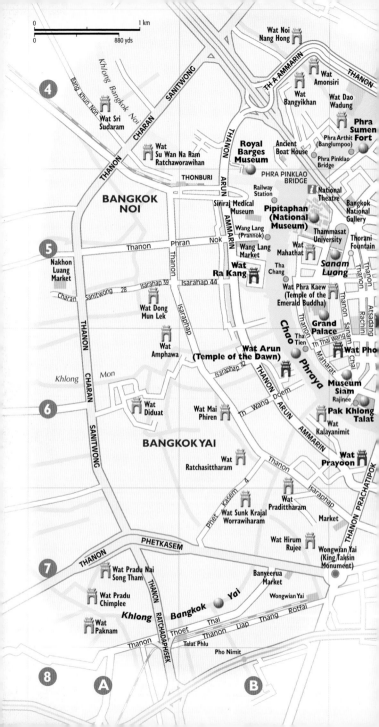

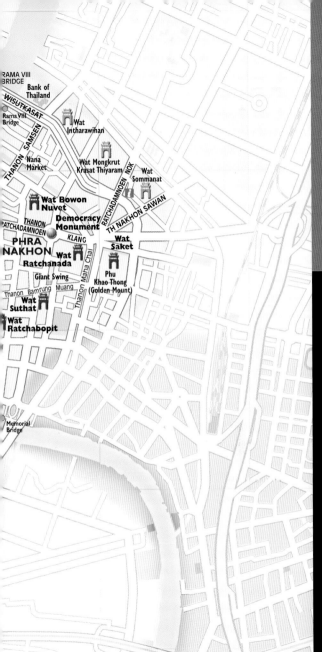

RAMA VIII
BRIDGE
Bank of
Thailand
WISUTKASAT
Rama VIII
Bridge
THANON SAMSEN
Nana
Market
Wat
Intharawihan
Wat Mongkrut
Krasat Thiyaram
Wat
Sommanat
RATCHADAMNOEN NOK
TH NAKHON SAWAN
Wat Bowon
Nuvet
THANON
RATCHADAMNOEN
Democracy
Monument
KLANG
PHRA
NAKHON
Wat
Ratchanada
Wat
Saket
Thanon Maha Chai
Giant Swing
Phu
Khao Thong
(Golden Mount)
Thanon Bamrung Muang
Wat
Suthat
Wat
Ratchabopit
Memorial
Bridge

C
D
E

Rattanakosin and Around

Grand Palace

HIGHLIGHTS

● Chakri Maha Prasad
● The garden
● Wat Phra Kaew Museum
● Amarin Vinichai Prasad
(Coronation Hall)
● Dusit Maha Prasad

TIP

● Ignore anyone around the Grand Palace who, telling you that it is closed for the day, offers what will turn out to be a shopping tour of the city.

The palace, home to the Thai royal family until 1946, is undoubtedly grand, with so many jewels crammed into a small area. The effect is overwhelming.

The oldest building When King Rama I moved from Thonburi to Rattanakosin his plan was to construct an exact copy of Ayutthaya. First he built himself a palace and a royal temple, Wat Phra Kaew. The oldest buildings are the Maha Montien and the Dusit Maha Prasad, the first brick building (1789) constructed in typical Thai style. It is now the resting place for deceased royals before their cremation.

The foreigner The magnificent Chakri Maha Prasad, designed by British architects, is often referred to as "the *farang* (foreigner) with the

chada (headdress worn by Thai dancers)," as the main building, in imperial Victorian style, is topped with three Thai spires. The ground level houses a display of weapons, while on the next level are the Throne Hall and Reception Hall. Only the weapons display is open to the public.

Emerald Buddha Within the Grand Palace grounds is the stunning Wat Phra Kaew (the Temple of the Emerald Buddha). It is the holiest of Thai wats, and the small green-jade statue of the Buddha, high on its golden altar in the Chapel Royal, is the most sacred image in Thailand. The late Ayutthaya-style murals on the surrounding walls depict the lives of Buddha, while the superb door panels, with mother-of-pearl inlay, illustrate scenes from the *Ramakien*, the Thai version of the *Ramayana*.

THE BASICS

royalgrandpalace.th
* B5–C5
* ✉ Thanon Na Phra Lan
* 🕐 Daily 8.30–3.30
* 🚢 Tha Chang
* ♿ Good
* 🎟 Moderate; includes Grand Palace, Queen Sirikit Textile Museum, Wat Phra Kaew and Vimanmek Palace. Tickets may be bought online
* ❓ Modest dress—no shorts, vests, short skirts, flip-flops or sandals (without ankle straps). Clothes can be rented at the office. Audio guides available

Mae Nam Chao Phraya

HIGHLIGHTS

● Several *wats*, including Wat Arun
● Grand Palace
● Several hotels, including the Oriental
● 19th-century buildings
● Rice barges being towed to and from Bangkok's port
● People living alongside the river
● Fresher air, a breeze and no traffic jams

The Chao Phraya River, Bangkok's main artery, was called the "River of Kings" by King Rama I. To board a boat, smell the breeze and see the grand buildings lining the banks is one of the most exhilarating experiences in Bangkok.

The river of kings You can learn much about the history of Bangkok from the Chao Phraya, for the city was designed to be seen from the water: A hundred years ago you would have arrived upriver from the sea port rather than across the city from the airport. Besides the Grand Palace (▷ 24–25), look out for other royal buildings: the Royal Barges Museum (▷ 30–31), Chakrabongse House, Wat Arun (▷ 32–33), Wat Ra Kang (▷ 38–39), Silpakorn University and, between Krung Thon

Clockwise from left: Wat Arun temple on the west bank of the river; riverside dining; aerial view across the river, with Wat Arun in the foreground

and Phra Pokklao bridges, the childhood home of Queen Sirikit.

The river of the people The more congested road traffic becomes, the more people in Bangkok dream of returning to their river. Many inhabitants still live waterborne lives in stilt houses and on barges, dependent on the brown river for their washing, fishing and transportation. Some people living on barges trade in charcoal, while others work at the rice warehouses across the river. Farther upstream, look for market traders around Pak Khlong Talat and teak loggers with their goods moored around Krung Thon Bridge. Life carries on as it has for centuries, with only a tidemark on some buildings to mark the devastating flood of fall 2011, when hundreds of people lost their lives.

THE BASICS

➕ B6

🍴 Excellent restaurants and bars

🚢 Public express boats, private long-tail boats

♿ None

❓ The Chao Phraya Express Boat Company (chaophrayaexpressboat. com) offers special tours on its boats and a map of the sights along the way. Info Center at Central Pier (Tha Saphan Taksin)

Pak Khlong Talat

TOP 25

Exotic blooms in all colors and for all occasions are sold at Pak Khlong Talat

THE BASICS

- ✚ C6
- ✉ Chakkaraphet Road, near Memorial Bridge
- 🕐 Daily 24 hours but busiest at night
- 🍴 Foodstalls
- 🚢 Tha Saphan Phut
- ♿ None
- 🎫 Free

DID YOU KNOW?

● There are more than 25,000 species of orchid documented, making it the largest family of flowering plants.
● Orchids can live up to 100 years but patience is required—flowering takes place between five and seven years after germination.
● Despite being thought of as "tropical," orchids grow on every continent.

Visit Thailand's biggest flower market by night to immerse yourself in the vibrant colors and heady scents of the intoxicating displays. Flowers are an integral part of life for Thais, largely due to their significance as offerings at temples and key times of celebration.

Displays of color The market moved indoors in 2016 but remains located on Chakkaraphet Road, where every night collections of roses, delicate orchids and carnations spill over onto adjacent stalls and shophouses. You can find an extraordinary range of flowers here, both home-grown in Thailand and imported. Flowers such as Dutch roses, tulips and, of course, orchids are sold at low prices. Moreover, there are flower arrangement services as well as ornamental flowers used in formal displays or bouquets and bows. Stallholders shop all over the kingdom to create breathtaking displays.

For business, for pleasure The market is both a wholesale and retail operation, so locals and visitors browse and buy alongside those making purchases to resell in flower shops across the city. Understandably, at key festive occasions and around Valentine's Day, Pak Khlong Talat is especially vibrant and prices soar. It's not all floral offerings here either. By day, Pak Khlong Talat is a wholesale produce market bursting with bundles of lemongrass, displays of colorful chilies and fresh herbs, galangal and Thai basil.

Pipitaphan (National Museum)

The museum buildings (below); stone figures on the exterior (right)

You'll need as long as possible to come to terms with this astonishing collection of Thai art and archaeology. Most of the museum's buildings, too, are works of art in their own right.

Oldest letters The visit starts with a useful introduction to Thai history. Note the black-stone inscription from Sukhothai, the oldest-known record of the Thai alphabet. Two modern buildings house the main collection of pre-Thai and Thai sculpture, as well as pieces from elsewhere in Asia. An important exhibit in the southern wing is one of the earliest images of Buddha, from Gandhara in India. A garage in a nearby building houses the collection of magnificent royal funeral chariots, including the amazing *Vejayant Rajarot*, built by Rama I in 1785 and still occasionally used, even though it needs 300 men to pull it.

Palace of Wang Na Built in the 1780s as a home for the king's successor, the palace houses a magnificent collection of Thai art objects. Note the collection of traditional musical instruments from Southeast Asia.

Buddhaisawan Chapel The Phra Sihing Buddha here is said to have been divinely created in Sri Lanka and sent to Sukhothai in the 13th century. Despite doubts about its origins (it dates from the 15th century), it is still worshiped by many and is carried in procession at the Thai New Year.

THE BASICS

- B5
- Thanon Naphratad 1
- 0 2224 1370
- Usually Wed–Sun 9–4, but check in advance
- Café
- Tha Phra Chan
- Few
- Inexpensive
- Free tours in English, German, French and Japanese take place every Wed and Thu at 9.30

HIGHLIGHTS

- Sukhothai sculpture
- *Vejayant Rajarot* chariot
- Red House
- Royal funeral chariots
- Murals in the Buddhaisawan Chapel

TIP

- Photography is not allowed inside the museum.

Royal Barges Museum

HIGHLIGHTS

● *Suphannahong*, the largest of the royal barges
● The serpent-headed prow of *Anantanagaraj*
● View along Khlong Bangkok Noi

TIP

● If your time is limited, join a river tour from the River City Shopping Complex.

Thai kings regularly used these splendidly carved barges, but now they are only taken out during the barge procession. This event marks a nonannual, auspicious Buddhist calendar year.

Fit for a king These superb boats are a reminder that Bangkok was once all canals. The most majestic is the king's personal barge, the *Suphannahong*, or the golden swan, which was the mythical steed of the Hindu god Brahma. The 148ft (45m) longboat is intricately carved from the trunk of a single teak tree and its prow rears up into a swanlike bird, known as the *hongsa*. The barge, manned by 50 oarsmen, was launched by King Rama VI in 1911. The second-largest barge in the shed is the *Anantanagaraj*. It is beautifully carved and has

a seven-headed *naga* serpent at its prow. Around it are others from the royal fleet—when 19th-century Thai kings ventured out, they were accompanied by hundreds of vessels.

The Royal Barge Procession No new royal barges have been built, but the spectacular pageant on water still occasionally takes place. Originally, the large fleet of royal barges aligned on the rivers and canals at the island capital of Ayutthaya at the end of the rainy season, when the king offered new robes for the monks at the royal monasteries. This event is still the main reason for the procession, but only in auspicious years. However, it can take place to celebrate another event, such as King Bhumibol's birthday in 2012 when 52 barges set sail—a majestic sight on the water.

THE BASICS

+ B4

✉ 80/1 Soi Rim Khlong Bangkok Noi

☎ 0 2424 0004

🕐 Daily 9–5

🚤 Chao Phraya Express boat to Tha Wang Lang and then taxi to museum

♿ Few

💷 Inexpensive

Wat Arun

HIGHLIGHTS

● Central *prang*
● Close-up of the Chinese porcelain decoration on the *prangs*
● Main Buddha image inside the *bot*
● Murals inside the *bot*

TIP

● Boat tours restrict your time at Wat Arun but the cross-river ferries are frequent and give you more freedom.

Despite the competition from many skyscrapers on Bangkok's skyline, the glittering towers of the Temple of Dawn rise tall above the river.

The temple of Arun King Taksin chose this 17th-century wat for his royal temple and palace as it was the first place in Thonburi to catch the morning light. The Emerald Buddha was housed here after it was recaptured from Laos before being moved to Wat Phra Kaew in 1785. Even without the sacred statue, Wat Arun continued to be revered, and kings Rama II and Rama III reconstructed and enlarged it to its present height of 220ft (67m). Today, the wat has a long, elongated, Khmer-style *prang* (tower), and four minor towers, symbolizing Mount Meru, the terrestrial representation of

From far left: The towering prang of Wat Arun is covered with Chinese porcelain; monks visit the wat; a statue decorated with an offering

the 33 heavens. The *prangs* are covered with pieces of porcelain, which Chinese boats coming to Bangkok used as ballast.

The main *prang* Steep steps lead to the two terraces that form the base of the *prang*. The different layers, or heavens, are supported by *kinnari*, or half-humans, and frightening *yak-shas*, or demons. Pavilions on the first platform contain statues of the Buddha at important stages of his life, while on the second terrace four statues of the Hindu god Indra stand guard.

Quiet stroll Stroll around the compound and have a look at the interior of the *bot* (chapel). The main Buddha image inside is believed to have been designed by Rama II himself, but the murals date from the reign of Rama V.

THE BASICS

watarun.net

➕ B6

✉ 34 Thanon Arun Amarin, Bangkok Yai

🕐 Daily 8.30–5.30

🍴 Foodstalls on the riverbank

🚢 Express boat to Tha Tien pier, then cross-river ferry to Wat Arun

♿ None

💷 Inexpensive

Wat Pho

**After a visit to the Grand Palace or a
day's shopping, there's nothing as relaxing as a visit to the beautiful temple
compound of Wat Pho and a good Thai
massage to get you back on your feet.**

The Reclining Buddha Wat Pho was built in
the 16th century during the Ayutthaya period
and almost completely rebuilt in 1781 by
Rama I. It is Bangkok's oldest and Thailand's
largest wat. Thanon Chetuphon divides the
grounds in two; only the northern part is open
to the public. The temple's main attraction is
the 19th-century giant Reclining Buddha, 151ft
(46m) long and 49ft (15m) high, which represents the dying Buddha in the position he
adopted to attain nirvana. The soles of the feet
are decorated in mother-of-pearl with 108 signs

of Buddha. The beautiful *bot*, or central shrine, has delicately carved sandstone panels representing the *Ramakien* and the finest mother-of-pearl inlaid doors. Although Wat Pho contains 91 *chedis*, the four most important are dedicated to the first Chakri kings. Visitors can acquire merit by putting a coin in each of the 108 bronze bowls.

Center of learning Rama III wanted this temple to be used for education, and Thais still consider it their first public university. The murals in the *viharn* and other buildings explain a variety of subjects, such as religion, geography, yoga, astrology, science and arts. Today, the temple complex still includes the traditional Thai Massage School (▷ 44), which teaches the art of Thai massage and herbal remedies.

THE BASICS

watpho.com
✚ C6
✉ 2 Thanon Sanam Chai
☎ 0 2226 0335
🕐 Daily 8–6.30, massage 8–5
🚢 Tha Tien pier
♿ Good
👋 Moderate

Wat Prayoon

This temple complex in the shadow of the old Memorial Bridge is dominated by a surreal artificial hill—covered with miniature shrines and overlooking a turtle pool—and its giant white pagoda.

Distinctive pagodas Wat Prayoon, also called Temple of the Dawn and known locally under its longer name of Wat Prayun Rawongsawat, was built during the reign of Rama III by the powerful local Bunnag family. Its huge *chedis* (pagodas) are easily recognized from the river and Memorial Bridge. In 2007, the large white pagoda at the back of the temple compound underwent a huge renovation, during which a cache of amulets and statues were found, which are now displayed next door. The wat has some fine mother-of-pearl inlaid doors.

From left: Turtle Mount is dotted about with shrines of all kinds and has a grotto at its base; the brilliant white Ayutthaya-style *chedi* in the main complex is the largest in Bangkok

Turtle Mount To the right as you enter the complex is a huge artificial hill, circled clockwise by worshipers. It was constructed by King Rama III after he observed the shapes made by candle wax as it melted and slowly drooped. Between the strange shapes are shrines to people's deceased loved ones in different sizes and styles, from the most traditional Thai pagoda-style *chedi* to a cowboy ranch complete with cacti. The thousands of turtles, of many different types, in the pond surrounding the shrines gave the mount its name. Vendors sell bread and papaya for visitors to feed these feted creatures—some locals believe special merit is gained by feeding them. At the edge of the pond is a memorial to the unfortunate men who died in 1836 when one of the temple's cannons exploded.

THE BASICS

🚩 C6

✉ Soi 1, off Thanon Thetsaban, Thonburi

🕐 Daily 6–5.30

🚢 Tha Saphan Phut Memorial Bridge

♿ None

✋ Free; inexpensive turtle food

Wat Ra Kang

*Wall paintings (left
and middle); the
gardens (below)*

THE BASICS

watrakang.com
🔲 B5
✉ Soi Wat Rakang
Khositaram, off Thanon
Arun Amarin
🕐 Daily 7am–9pm
🚤 Express boat to
Tha Chang pier, then
cross-river ferry to Wat
Ra Kang pier
♿ None
🖐 Free

HIGHLIGHTS

● Woodcarvings in the
library
● Murals of the *Ramakien*
● Views of the Grand
Palace

**Claims that the Ayutthaya period was
one of the high points of Thai art are
supported by this undervisited temple,
set on the banks of the Chao Phraya
River. Its murals and woodcarvings are
exceptionally fine.**

Bell temple Most visitors overlook this
delightful smaller wat, which dates from the
Ayutthaya period like its neighbor, Wat Arun
(▷ 32–33). King Taksin undertook serious res-
torations when he settled in Thonburi, and
Rama I rebuilt it extensively. *Rakang* means
bell, and visitors can ring the bells to bring good
luck. The lovely garden feels far removed from
bustling Bangkok and is a great place to rest, to
enjoy the cross-river view of the Grand Palace,
or even to meditate.

A royal present The beautiful library on the
compound of Wat Ra Kang was a gift from
Rama I to the temple after he founded the
Chakri Dynasty. He lived in this elegant 18th-
century teak building before he became king,
and carried out extensive renovations at the
time. The stucco and carved wooden doors and
window panels are incredibly fine examples of
the Ayutthaya style, depicting figures from the
epic *Ramakien*, the Thai interpretation of the
Indian Hindu *Ramayana* story. Both the doors
and the murals on the interior walls—the work
of the great priest-painter Phra Acharn Nak—are
considered by art historians to be among the
finest in Bangkok.

Wat Saket

A decorated window (below); the Golden Mount (right)

It's easy to get lost in the grounds of this vast, peaceful temple, but the short, steep climb up the Golden Mount puts everything in perspective and offers great views over Rattanakosin and the city.

Golden Mount The main attraction here is the Golden Mount (Phu Khao Thong). The artificial hill, nearly 262ft (80m) high, was created in the early 19th century after a large *chedi* built by Rama III collapsed when the underlying ground gave way. Only a huge pile of rubble was left, but as Buddhists believe that a religious building should never be destroyed, King Rama IV had 1,000 teak logs put into the foundations. Later, Rama V built a small *chedi* on top of the hill, which is believed to contain Buddha's teeth. During World War II, concrete walls were added to halt erosion. Views from the terrace on top of the hill are wonderful, and you are allowed into the golden *chedi*.

Temple complex The temple was built outside the city walls by King Rama I during the late 18th century as the city's main crematorium. The king performed the Royal Hair Bathing Ceremony here before he was crowned. When plague raged through the city in the 19th century, the temple became a charnel house to tens of thousands of victims. The temple building itself is not very interesting, but the fine murals inside the main temple are worth a close inspection. There are two important old Buddha statues in the Shrine Hall.

THE BASICS

✚ D5
✉ Between Boriphat Road and Lan Luang Road, off Ratchadamnoen Klang Road; best reached by metered taxi
☎ 0 2223 4561
🕓 Daily 8–4
♿ None
👑 Free; donation for top of Golden Mount

HIGHLIGHTS

● Views over Rattanakosin
● Murals in the main chapel
● Tiny bird and antiques market
● Candle-lit procession up the Golden Mount late October/early November

More to See

DEMOCRACY MONUMENT

This art deco monument was constructed in 1932 to commemorate Thailand's transformation from an absolute to a constitutional monarchy. The 75 cannon balls buried in the base refer to the Buddhist Year 2475, which is 1932, and the four wings stand 78ft (24m) tall, representing June 24 when the constitution was signed.

🚩 C5 ✉ Thanon Ratchadamnoen Klang
🚢 Tha Phra Athit

MUSEUM SIAM

museumsiam.org

Located in a renovated colonial building, this interactive museum depicts the history of Thailand in a fresh and innovative way. Kids will love the opportunity to dress up.

🚩 C6 ✉ Thanon Sanam Chai ☎ 0225 2777 🕐 Tue–Sun 10–6 🚢 Rajinee pier
💷 Expensive

PHRA SUMEN FORT

Dating from 1783, this is one of the 14 city fortresses built to protect the city against naval invasions. The octagonal structure is surrounded by the small Santichaiprakan Park. A walkway leads from the fort to the Phra Pin Klao Bridge, allowing you to peek inside some of the old buildings. The area of Banglamphu takes its name from the Lamphu or Engler Tree. Only one of these trees, a mangrove plant which grew all along the river, survives and is in the park.

🚩 C4 ✉ Thanon Phra Athit 🕐 Daily 24 hours 🚢 Tha Phra Athit

SANAM LUANG

Just north of the Grand Palace are the royal cremation grounds, today most often used for picnics. The whole area is a good place to relax after sightseeing or to watch kite competitions, which usually take place between February and May. The last ceremonial cremation, attended by thousands of people, took place in October 2017 for the funeral of King Bhumibol Adulyadej

Learn about Thailand in an interesting and fun way at Museum Siam

Four wings surround the Democracy Monument

(Rama IX). The lovely Lak Muang (City Pillar Shrine) is believed to be inhabited by the spirit that protects the city of Bangkok and is often the site of displays of traditional Thai dance (▷ 44). Every day Thais come to the temple to leave offerings of food and flower garlands and to pray.

🔳 B5–C5 🖂 Thanon Ratchadamnoen Nai 🕐 Daily morning–evening 🚢 Express boat to Tha Chang and then 10-minute walk 🎫 Free

WAT BOWON NUVET

watbowon.org

This temple houses the Phra Phutthachinnasi, a very beautiful Buddha image molded around 1357. The temple is considered one of Bangkok's most important temples as King Rama IV was chief abbot here before he ascended the throne. King Bhumibol stayed for a short time in 1956.

🔳 C5 🖂 Thanon Phra Sumen, Banglamphu ☎ 0 2281 2831 🕐 Daily 8–5 🚢 Tha Phra Athit 🎫 Free 🚹 Dress appropriately

WAT RATCHANADA

The strangest structure on this temple compound is Loha Prasad, or the Iron Monastery, a pink building with metal spires, spectacularly lit at night. Bangkok's biggest amulet market is held daily nearby.

🔳 C5 🖂 Off Thanon Maha Chai, opposite Wat Saket ☎ 0 2224 8807 🕐 Daily 8–5 🍴 Foodstalls 🚢 Express ferry to Tha Chang pier and then *tuk-tuk* 🎫 Free

WAT SUTHAT

Wat Suthat houses a 14th-century Buddha statue surrounded by depictions of the Buddha's last 24 lives. The courtyard is filled with old statues of scholars and sailors, brought as ballast in rice boats, while the doors of the wat are said to have been carved by Rama II. In an annual ceremony for the rice harvest, men used to ride on the Giant Swing and try to grab a bag of silver coins hanging from a pole.

🔳 C5 🖂 Off Thanon Bamrung Muang ☎ 0 2224 9845 🕐 Daily 8.30am–9pm 🍴 Foodstalls 🚢 Tha Chang

Three images of Buddha on the exterior of Wat Suthat

Rattanakosin
(Royal City)

See where it all began, with the grandest of the city's temples, street markets, a park and maybe a relaxing massage on the way.

DISTANCE: 2 miles (3km) **ALLOW:** 3 hours

START

MAHA RAT PIER
🔲 B5 🚢 Tha Maha Rat

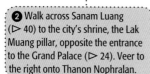

1 From Maha Rat pier, turn right on Thanon Maharat and then left on Drok Sillapakorn. The entrance to the old temple complex, Wat Mahathat, is on the left, opposite Sanam Luang.

2 Walk across Sanam Luang (▷ 40) to the city's shrine, the Lak Muang pillar, opposite the entrance to the Grand Palace (▷ 24). Veer to the right onto Thanon Nophralan.

3 Make a left turn on Thanon Maharat to stroll through the street markets. Past the palace, on the left-hand side, you can see Wat Pho (▷ 34).

4 Here you can have a massage (▷ 44). Walk along Thanon Chetuphon, take a left on busy Thanon Sanam Chai, then right onto Thanon Sararom.

END

DEMOCRACY MONUMENT
🔲 C5 🚢 Tha Phra Athit

8 Head along Thanon Din So toward the Democracy Monument (▷ 40), which is now a chaotic traffic circle (roundabout).

7 Continue on the same street and make a left turn on Thanon Ti Thong, with its local shops. At the intersection with Thanon Bamrung Muang, explore the wonderful Wat Suthat (▷ 41) and the nearby Giant Swing.

6 Cross the canal by the footbridge to Thanon Ratchabopit, with yet another temple, Wat Ratchabopit, to the right.

5 Wat Ratchapradit is on the right and there is a bizarre sculpture of a pig at the end of the street.

RATTANAKOSIN AND AROUND WALK

42

Shopping

AMULET MARKET

Stalls and small shops at this outdoor market sell all kinds of amulets, from the obvious images of Buddha and famous monks and abbots to rare and valuable relics. Collectors hover over the stalls with keen concentration.

⊞ B5 ⊠ Across Wat Mahathat temple, off Thanon Maharat 🚢 Tha Chang

ELEPHANT HOUSE

elephant-house.com

This shop has a selection of furniture and artifacts made from traditional materials such as rattan, bamboo and lacquerware. Everything sold here is designed by the owner, Cherie Aung-Khin, and brought to life by her skilled craftsmen.

⊞ C7 ⊠ 230/27 Soi Krungthonburi 6, Krungthonburi Road 🕿 0 2860 6920 🚇 Skytrain Krung Thonburi

LOFTY BAMBOO

loftybamboo.com

This is a fun shop selling gifts, bags, clothes and jewelry made by the Hmong, Lisu and Akha hill tribes. Outlets such as Lofty Bamboo encourage the continuity of these traditional skills and ensure that the villagers get a fair price for their work.

⊞ C5 ⊠ G–10 1st Floor Buddy Hotel, 265 Thanon Khao San, Talatyot, Phranakorn 🕿 0 2629 4716 🚢 Tha Phra Athit

NITTAYA CURRY SHOP

Nittaya's curry pastes are considered Thailand's best and her well-sealed curry pots make a perfect souvenir or gift. You can try out the preparations at the gift and snack session before you buy.

⊞ C5 ⊠ Thanon Chakkaphong 136–140, Banglamphu 🕿 0 2976 1600 🚢 Tha Phra Athit

SHAMAN BOOKS

shaman-books.tripod.com

This new and used bookshop stocks a vast range of novels, guide books, Buddhist titles and Asian travel literature.

⊞ C5 ⊠ 71 Thanon Khao San 🕿 0 2629 0418 🚢 Tha Phra Athit

TAEKEE TAEKON

At Taekee Taekon the prices are more or less fixed—expect around a 10 percent discount—and there is a reasonable choice of quality textiles, silk items, axe cushions, jewelry, baskets, various stationery items as well as bags.

⊞ C4 ⊠ 118 Thanon Phra Athit 🕿 0 2629 1473 🚢 Tha Phra Athit

THANON KHAO SAN MARKET

The stalls and shops here are piled high with everything possible that shoppers may need and more. Expect to find henna tattooing, hemp clothing, fairy lights, T-shirts, fresh orange juice, banana pancakes and a raft of fake designer wear. Also, if you have time, check out the alleyways away from the main thoroughfare, which have many other interesting shops.

⊞ C5 ⊠ Thanon Khao San 🚢 Tha Phra Athit

SILVER PARADISE

The eastern end of Thanon Khao San and Thanon Tanao has become an area specializing in wholesale jewelry, and sterling silver in particular. Amazing silver beads, pendants and jewelry designs can be found here at just a little more than wholesale prices. Most items are sold by weight, and by the amount of craftsmanship involved. Don't be afraid to haggle: start by offering 25 percent less than the asking price with a view to achieving 10–15 percent off.

Entertainment and Nightlife

BROWN SUGAR

brownsugarbangkok.com

Brown Sugar: The Jazz Boutique has been around since the 1980s and continues to draw great bands six evenings a week. The Brown Sugar Sunday Special, every Sunday at 10.30pm, showcases up-and-coming international and touring artists.

➕ C5 ✉ 469 Wanchad Junction, Thanon Phrasumen, Baworniet ☎ 0 2282 0396 🕐 Tue–Thu, Sun 5pm–1am, Fri–Sat 5pm–1am 🚉 Tha Phra Athit

THE CLUB KHAOSAN

theclubkhaosan.com

Whatever your favorite sound—be it progressive, electro, trance or house—resident and international DJs pump it out across the large dance floor with their state-of-the-art sound system. Live bands also perform here.

➕ C5 ✉ 123 Thanon Khao San, Talat Yot, Phra Nakhon ☎ 0 2629 1010 🕐 Daily 10pm–3am 🚉 Tha Phra Athit

JAZZ HAPPENS

An intimate setting a stone's throw from the hustle and bustle of Khao San Road belies the caliber of the musical talent on display here. Cool, unpretentious and popular with young Thais, this is a great place to spot young jazz talent over some food and drinks.

➕ C5 ✉ 62 Phra Athit Road ☎ 0 4450 0505 🕐 Daily 5pm–1am 🚉 Tha Phra Athit then walk (or taxi/tuk-tuk)

LAK MUANG

Thai dancers perform classical dances several times a day on a special stage at this shrine (▷ 41), which commemorates the founding of Bangkok.

➕ B–C5 ✉ Thanon Ratchadamnoen Nai 🕐 Daily 8.30–3.30 🚉 Tha Phra Chan

MAY KAIDEE COOKERY CLASS

maykaidee.com/cooking-school

Long-established vegetarian cookery school with morning or afternoon sessions. Students learn about Thai herbs and spices, how to make spring rolls and classic Thai dishes such as Pad Thai—and then eat the results.

➕ C5 ✉ 59 Tanao Road, Banglamphu ☎ 0 2629 4413 🕐 Daily; classes begin at 9am or 2pm 🚉 Tha Phra Athit

MULLIGANS IRISH BAR

Head to this popular venue to watch live international sport on TV and enjoy a refreshing pint of Guinness with classic pub food, Irish stew or Thai snacks. There's live music in the upstairs bar every day except Sunday.

➕ C5 ✉ 265 Thanon Khao San, Talat Yot, Phra Nakhon ☎ 0 2629 4477 🕐 Daily 24 hours 🚉 Tha Phra Aphit

RATCHADAMNOEN STADIUM

This is one of the main venues for *Muay Thai* (Thai Boxing), an exciting sport which utilizes every part of the body to fend off an opponent.

➕ D4 ✉ Thanon Ratchadamnoen Nok ☎ 0 2281 4205 🕐 Mon, Wed, Thu 6.30pm, Sun 5pm 🚉 Skytrain Phaya Thai then taxi

WAT PHO THAI TRADITIONAL MASSAGE SCHOOL

watpomassage.com

Come here for a good, inexpensive massage by experienced, if nonsmiling, masseurs. This excellent school also offers professional Thai massage courses for visitors who are here longer, including foot massage, spa treatments and advanced medical massage.

➕ C6 ✉ Thanon Sanam Chai ☎ 0 2662 3533 🕐 Courses from 1 to 5 weeks; massages daily 8–5 🚉 Tha Tien

Where to Eat

PRICES
Prices are approximate, based on a 3-course meal for one person.
$$$ more than 2,000B
$$ 1,000B–2,000B
$ under 1,000B

ERR ($$)

errbkk.com

The mission of this charming place close to the Grand Palace is to deliver an "urban rustic Thai experience" based on a close relationship with local farmers and artisanal producers. The menu is curated by Bo and Dylan of the Michelin-starred Bo.Lan.

🔹 C5/C6 ✉ 394/35 Maharaj Road ☎ 0 2622 2291 🕐 Tue–Sun 11–9.30 🚤 Tha Thien

DECK BY THE RIVER ($$)

arunresidence.com

Reservations are necessary at this idyllic outdoor restaurant set on a deck by the river with views across to Wat Arun. Early evening is popular as the sun sets.

🔹 B5 ✉ 36–38 Soi Pratoo Nok Young, Thanon Maharat ☎ 0 2221 9158 🕐 Mon–Thu 11–10, Fri–Sun 11am–1am 🚤 Tha Thien

HEMLOCK ($–$$)

Small but charming, Hemlock is frequented by Thai artists and writers as well as those who work nearby. The menu is extensive, with excellent dishes from all over the country.

🔹 C4 ✉ Thanon Phra Athit 56, Banglamphu ☎ 0 2282 7507 🕐 Mon–Fri 4pm–midnight, Sat 5pm–midnight 🚤 Tha Phra Athit

MAY KAIDEE'S VEGETARIAN RESTAURANT ($)

maykaidee.com

Tucked away down a lane, parallel to but behind Thanon Tanao, this small but friendly place is worth seeking out for its inexpensive green curry, carrot salad, fried water spinach and other vegetarian delights. The best dessert is the black sticky rice with coconut milk, banana and mango.

🔹 C5 ✉ 59 Thanon Tanao (near Thanon Khao San) ☎ 0 2629 4413 🕐 Daily 9am–10pm 🚤 Tha Phra Athit

SEVEN SPOONS ($)

sevenspoonsbkk.wordpress.com

In a restored Chinese shophouse, this minimalist gastrobar serves contemporary cuisine with a Mediterranean twist.

🔹 D5 ✉ 22–24 Chakkrapatipong ☎ 0 2629 9214 🕐 Tue–Sat 11–3 and 6pm–1am, Sun 6pm–1am 🚤 Tha Phra Athit then *tuk-tuk*

SHEEPSHANK PUBLIC HOUSE ($–$$)

sheepshankpublichouse.com

Modern American cuisine is on the menu in this converted boat repair shop with great views of the river. The prices are great and there's not a burger in sight!

🔹 C4 ✉ Thanon Phra Athit 47, Chana Songkram, Phra Nakhon ☎ 0 2629 5165 🕐 Tue–Sun 6pm–midnight 🚤 Tha Phra Athit

HIGH TEA
The Chinese claim that hot tea is the best way to cool down and to recover from the heat. English tea is something of an institution in Bangkok. The traditional place to take it is the Author's Lounge in the Mandarin Oriental Hotel (▷ 58, 112), but the grand lobbies of the Four Seasons (▷ 112), and the Shangri-La Hotel and Peninsula (▷ 112) also offer teatime buffets accompanied by uplifting classical music. The Banyan Tree (▷ 112) serves high tea or a Thai tiffin box.

Silom, Surawong and Chinatown

Bangkok's bustling business area has wholesalers in the alleys of Chinatown, and the towers of the major banks on Silom and Sathorn roads. In the middle of it all are temples, museums and sights.

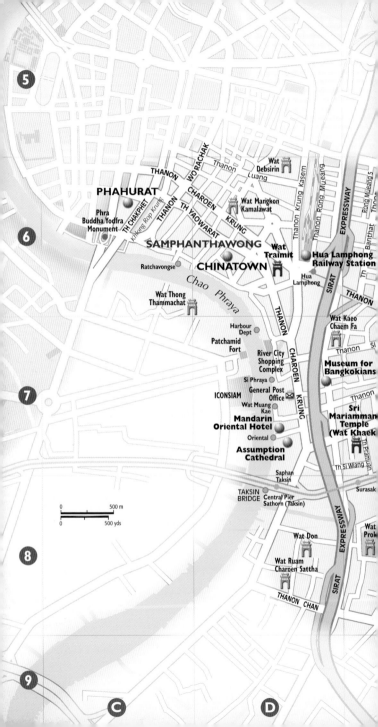

5

6

7

8

9

THANON

WO RACHAK

Thanon

Wat
Debsirin

PHAHURAT

THANON

CHAROEN

TH CHAKPHET

TH YAOWARAT

Wat Mangkon
Kamalawat

Phra
Buddha Yodfra
Monument

Khlong Rop Krung

KRUNG

Thanon Krung Kasem

Thanon Krung Mueang

Rong Mueang 5

Thanon

Thanon Rong Mueang

EXPRESSWAY

Banthat

SAMPHANTHAWONG

**Wat
Traimit**

**Hua Lamphong
Railway Station**

Ratchavongse

CHINATOWN

Hua
Lamphong

SIRAT

THANON

Chao Phraya

Wat Thong
Thammachat

THANON

Wat Kaeo
Chaem Fa

Harbour
Dept

CHAROEN

Thanon

Si

Patchamid
Fort

River City
Shopping
Complex

**Museum for
Bangkokians**

Si Phraya

Thanon

KRUNG

ICONSIAM

General Post
Office

**Sri
Mariamman
Temple
(Wat Khaek)**

Wat Muang
Kae

**Mandarin
Oriental Hotel**

Oriental

Th Pramuan

**Assumption
Cathedral**

Th Si Wiang

Saphan
Taksin

Surasak

**TAKSIN
BRIDGE**

Central Pier
Sathorn (Taksin)

Wat Don

EXPRESSWAY

Wat
Prok

Wat Ruam
Charoen Sattha

SIRAT

THANON CHAN

C

D

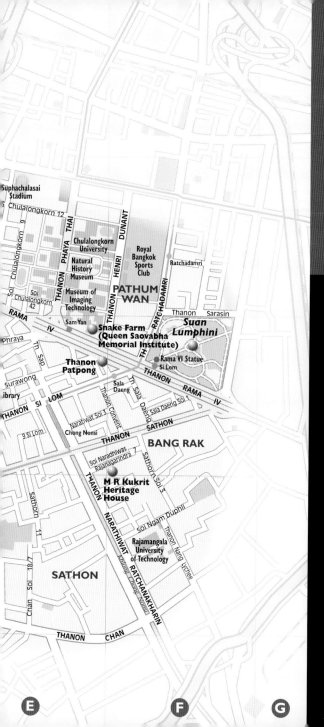

Suphachalasai
Stadium

Chulalongkorn 12

Chulalongkorn 9

Soi Chulalongkorn 42

Soi Chulalongkorn

THANON PHAYA THAI

Chulalongkorn
University

HENRI DUNANT

Natural
History
Museum

Museum of
Imaging
Technology

**PATHUM
WAN**

Royal
Bangkok
Sports
Club

Ratchadamri

RATCHADAMRI

RAMA IV

phraya

Th Sap

Sam Yan

THANON

**Snake Farm
(Queen Saovabha
Memorial Institute)**

Thanon Sarasin

*Suan
Lumphini*

surawong

ibrary

SI LOM

Th Si Lom

**Thanon
Patpong**

Rama VI Statue
Si Lom

Sala
Daeng

THANON RAMA IV

THANON SI LOM

Thanon Convent

Narathiwat Soi 3

Chong Nonsi

Th Sala Daeng

Sala Daeng

Sala Daeng Soi 1

Sathon Soi 3

THANON SATHON

BANG RAK

Sathon

THANON NARATHIWAT RATCHANAKHARIN

Soi Naradhiwas
Rajanagarindra 7

**M R Kukrit
Heritage
House**

Soi Ngam Duphli

Thanon Nang Lyntee

Rajamangala
University
of Technology

Khlong Chong Nonsi

Sathon 11

Chan Soi 18/7

SATHON

THANON CHAN

E   F   G

Chinatown

TOP 25

Chinatown's intricate alleys are crammed with tiny temples, shrouded in incense clouds, between ramshackle shophouses, food stalls and busy markets, while street vendors squeeze their laden carrying poles between pedestrians.

The Chinese community By the 14th century, Chinese merchants had set up vital trading centers in Thailand and were the only foreigners allowed to live within the walls of Ayutthaya. The Chinese were already well established in Bangkok when King Rama I built his capital on their grounds in 1782 and moved them to the Sampeng area. For a long time Chinatown was the city's commercial center, also gaining notoriety for its many brothels, teahouses and opium dens. The restored Sala

Clockwise from far left: Street vendor navigating a Chinatown market; at the heart of Chinatown is the Chinese-Buddhist temple of Wat Mangkon Kamalawat; the gateway leading to Wat Mangkon Kamalawat; Chinatown is just as lively by night

Chalermkrung Royal Theater (▷ 65) is a perfect example of the theaters in the area. Chinese temples seem more workaday than their Thai counterparts but the Leng Noi Yee (Dragon Lotus Temple, ▷ 60) is a riot of gold and crimson, bustling with locals making offerings, especially on high days and holidays. You will find old Chinese men playing chess and watching the crocodiles in Wat Chakrawat.

Street markets Chinatown reveals its true soul in its street markets, old shophouses and shopping streets. The busiest alleyways are Soi Wanit 1 (Sampeng Lane) and Soi Isaraphap, and through the heart of it all cuts Thanon Yaowarat, famous for its gold shops. For a bit of local color, stroll through the flower and vegetable market Pak Khlong Talat (▷ 28).

THE BASICS

✚ C6–D6

🍴 Street stalls along Thanon Yaowarat

🚇 Hua Lamphong

🚢 Tha Ratchawong

♿ Few

TIP

● Following the walk on page 60 minimizes the chances of losing your bearings amid the warren of small streets and narrow alleyways.

M.R. Kukrit Heritage House

HIGHLIGHTS

HIGHLIGHTS

● Thai-style pavilion
● Library
● Tropical gardens
● Art treasures, Buddhist images and vintage furniture

Former prime minister M.R. Kukrit lived in this house until 1995, and it is now one of the few places that gives an insight into traditional upper-class Thai life.

Calm haven Like Jim Thompson's House (▷ 72–73), Kukrit's home is a peaceful retreat from Bangkok's more frenetic attractions. The understated charm of the property is a key part of its appeal. Overshadowed by skyscrapers, the traditional compound comprises five teak houses, collected from other parts of Thailand and reassembled on site. Together they celebrate M.R. Kukrit's passion for traditional Thai culture, art, literature and design. Artifacts on display in the music, reading and living rooms include old Buddhist scriptures, rare books and gifts bestowed on him by China—two vases

From left: The separate pavilion was used for banquets and public functions; the buildings are surrounded by lush gardens, filled with exotic plants, ponds and the miniature trees Kukrit loved to cultivate

from Mao Zedong and a Chinese altar given by Deng Xiaoping. As is traditional in many Thai homes, the garden plays a pivotal role, providing a peaceful green retreat.

Man of many talents The great-grandson of King Rama II, Kukrit was born in 1911. Like many boys of his background, he was sent to complete his education in England, graduating from Oxford University. He entered politics after World War II, eventually becoming prime minister for just a year in 1975, but his true vocation was always for the arts. He wrote over 40 books, plays and poems and was named National Artist in Literature in 1985, as well as founding the Khon Thammasat Troupe (*khon* is regarded as the highest form of dance drama in Thai classical arts). He died in 1995.

THE BASICS

➕ F8

✉ 19 Soi Prapinit, South Sathorn Road

☎ 0 2287 2937

🕐 Daily 10–6

🚆 Skytrain Chong Nonsi

♿ None

🎫 Inexpensive

Snake Farm

The daily snake-handling demonstrations are always popular

THE BASICS

saovabha.com

🔢 E7

✉ 1871 Rama IV

☎ 0 2252 0161

🕐 Mon–Fri 8.30–4.30, Sat–Sun 9.30–12. Venom extraction: Mon–Fri 11. Snake-handling demonstration: Mon–Fri 2.30, Sat–Sun 11

🚆 Skytrain Sala Daeng

♿ None

👟 Moderate

HIGHLIGHTS

● Watching the scientists extract the snake venom
● Snake-handling demonstration
● Getting up close (but not too close) to a king cobra

Perhaps a surprising thing to find in the heart of Bangkok, the Snake Farm is a great place to get up close and personal to exotic snakes and learn more about these fascinating creatures.

A serious purpose Back in 1929, the Thai royal family agreed to support the work of the Thai Red Cross to establish a center of research into poisonous snakes and venom antidotes, linked with the Queen Saovabha Memorial Institute, which was originally established in 1913 to produce vaccines against rabies. The institute has a comprehensive educational program for both visitors and professionals, and also produces antivenom to treat humans who have been bitten by a venomous snake.

What to expect Around 35 venomous snakes, including cobras and pythons, live in well-maintained vivariums in the Simaseng building in the institute. In the specially constructed 100-seat arena there are regular snake-handling demonstrations by the scientists, who clearly have a passion for their work, and afterward visitors are given the opportunity to have their photo taken with the friendly boa constrictor. There are also demonstrations of venom extraction, which is needed to produce antivenoms. If you want to know more about snakes, there is also a museum in the Simaseng building with displays on the anatomy and life cycle of snakes—and what to do in the event of a snake bite.

Fountain displays on the lake (left); perfect spot for an evening picnic (right)

A small town in southern Nepal where the Buddha was born gives its name to this large park in downtown Bangkok, popular with locals for outdoor recreation. Spend time in this pulsating city and the value of Lumphini becomes apparent.

An oasis of calm It is a vast expanse of green within the buzzing city—a place to seek some respite from the frenzy of urban stress and enjoy some moments of peace and quiet.

First light Lumphini is a place of moods rather than sights. In the early morning, before 7am, the park is full of people exercising. The graceful, Chinese-led t'ai chi groups make slow movements to music. It all comes to an abrupt halt and everyone stands to attention when the PA system plays the national anthem. By 9am, when the sun is up and rush-hour traffic has started, the crowd thins out.

Last light There's a different crowd in the afternoon. Joggers run on the 1.5-mile (2.5km) track, people pump weights at the open-air gym, and, in the windy season (February to April), kites soar above the busy city—at the height of the season you can buy beautiful kites here. When the light softens so does the atmosphere. Couples come out, foodstalls are set up and boats are rowed on the artificial lake until, at 6pm, with traffic at a halt in the evening rush, people in the park also stand still as the national anthem is played again.

THE BASICS

- ✚ F7
- ✉ Bordered by Thanon Rama IV, Thanon Ratchadamri, Thanon Witthaya (Wireless Road) and Thanon Sarasin
- 🕐 Daily 4.30am–9pm
- 🍴 Restaurant and food-stalls on the north side
- 🚋 Skytrain Sala Daeng
- 🚇 Lumphini and Silom
- ♿ Very good
- 👆 Free

HIGHLIGHTS

- ● Enjoying the open space and fresh air away from the craziness that is Bangkok
- ● Joining in the early morning t'ai chi or late afternoon aerobic sessions.
- ● Spotting the large monitor lizards

TIP

- ● Check out the elevated walkway connecting Lumphini with Banjasiri Park, just under a mile (1.5km) away.

Wat Traimit

● Some of Thailand's finest art was produced during the Sukhothai period (13th–15th centuries).
● Sukhothai Buddhas are usually seated, with hands in the Bhumisparsa Mudra position, the right hand touching the earth and the left resting in the lap.

In a country where all Buddha images are treated with respect, imagine the horror when workmen moved a large Buddha and a lump of stucco fell off. The fortuitous outcome was the Temple of the Golden Buddha.

The Golden Buddha The shiny, 10ft-tall (3m) gold Buddha, which weighs a hefty 5.5 tons, is believed to be the largest golden Buddha image in the world. The sculpture, made in Sukhothai in the 13th century, was covered with stucco as a disguise to protect it from Burmese invaders in the 18th century. The disguise served the statue well, as it wasn't until 1955 that its true nature was discovered. A crane cable snapped while it was being moved to a new building, sending the statue

From left: The lavish exterior of Phra Maha Mondop; the Golden Buddha sits in splendor on the top floor of the mondop

crashing to the ground. When a monk spotted something shining through the resulting cracks, the stucco was taken off and the solid gold structure was revealed. The discovery sparked a national treasure hunt, but nothing else of similar value was found. It seems appropriate that the Golden Buddha has found its home in Chinatown, at the center of Bangkok's gold trade. The statue is now valued at hundreds of millions of dollars. Several bits of the old stucco are on display to the left of it.

A new home The Golden Buddha was moved to a new home in the temple grounds in 2010, the golden-spired Phra Maha Mondop. The upstairs exhibition explains the origins of the Buddha, how it was discovered and how it was moved to its new home.

THE BASICS

✚ D6

✉ Thanon Traimit, off Thanon Charoen Krung, Chinatown

☎ 0 2623 1227

🕐 Daily 8–5

🍴 Foodstalls in Chinatown

🚇 Hua Lamphong

♿ None

💷 Inexpensive

More to See

ASSUMPTION CATHEDRAL

assumption-cathedral.com

Its distinctive Western Romanesque architecture makes this cathedral, the most important Catholic church in Thailand, stand out. Built at the beginning of the 20th century, replacing an earlier 19th-century building, the classic exterior hides a more ornate interior, with high ceilings and colorful frescoes. Pope John Paul II visited in 1984 and his statue, outside the main door, welcomes the faithful.

🔂 D7 ✉ 23 Charoen Krung, Soi 40 ☎ 0 2234 8556 ⏲ During daylight hours; English mass Sunday 10am 🚊 Skytrain Saphan Taksin 🚇 Sathorn

HUA LAMPHONG RAILWAY STATION

A superb example of Thai-style art deco, the beautiful central railroad station was opened in 1916. It is due to close in 2019 and be converted into a museum.

🔂 D6 ✉ Thanon Phra Rama IV 🚇 Hua Lamphong

MANDARIN ORIENTAL HOTEL

mandarinoriental.com

There are hotels, and then there's the Oriental. Nothing remains of the original 1876 Oriental, but the colonial Authors' Residence is the surviving building of 1887. This section contains the most luxurious suites, named after such illustrious guests as Noel Coward, and continues to attract celebrities. The lounge is a great place to enjoy afternoon tea, while the luxurious spa offers every imaginable treat. There is also a world-class cookery school, and an excellent cultural program run by university professors.

🔂 D7 ✉ 48 Soi Oriental ☎ 0 2659 9000 🍴 Restaurants and bar 🚊 Skytrain Saphan Taksin (free shuttle boat to hotel from Sathorn pier) ⛴ Tha Oriental pier 👔 Smart-casual dress

MUSEUM FOR BANGKOKIANS

The daughter of the original owners of this beautiful house, set in tranquil gardens, opened it as a museum to give an insight into how

View through the lush gardens, toward the old part of the Mandarin Oriental Hotel

Assumption Cathedral

wealthy Thai people used to live in the postwar period. The main house, with louvred teak windows and polished wooden floors, was built in 1937. A second building, dating from 1929, was the home of a British-Indian doctor and a third contains a collection of miscellaneous objects and a photo gallery.

➕ D7 ✉ 273 Soi Charoen Krung off Thanon Charoen Krung ☎ 0 2233 7027 🕐 Tue–Sun 10–4 💲 Free

PHAHURAT

Phahurat is Bangkok's Little India. Most of the shops sell fabrics—everything from silk to furnishing fabrics—and gems. Just off Thanon Chakraphet is Sri Gurusingh Sabha, a Sikh temple with golden domes. Every day at 9am blessed food is offered to devotees.

➕ C6 ⛴ Tha Saphan Phut pier

SRI MARIAMMAN TEMPLE (WAT KHAEK)

Built during the 1860s, when many Indians arrived here rather than live in India under colonial British rule, this Hindu temple is dedicated to Shakti, consort of Shiva. It is a riot of colors and a great place for people-watching as worshipers come to make their offerings.

➕ E7 ✉ Corner of Thanon Silom and Thanon Pan ☎ 0 2238 4007 🕐 Daily 6am–8pm 🚇 Skytrain Chong Nonsi

THANON PATPONG

As much a curiosity for foreign visitors as a true red-light area, Patpong is renowned for its go-go bars and clubs. The two parallel streets and dead-end lane are regular shopping streets during the day but at night, with the arrival of food stalls and a tacky, but popular, night market filled with bootleg DVDs and fake designer watches, the area is transformed. Stick to the downstairs bars as some of the upper, less savory bars are known to overcharge.

➕ E7 ✉ Soi Patpong 1, 2, 3, 4 between Thanon Silom and Thanon Surawong 🚇 Skytrain Sala Daeng 🚇 Silom

Fabric shop in Phahurat market

Sri Mariamman Temple

Around Chinatown

Chinatown is busy, noisy and filled with exotic smells—all of which make a visit a sensory and cultural experience.

DISTANCE: 1.5 miles (2.5km) **ALLOW:** 3 hours

START

THA RATCHAWONG PIER
⊞ C6 🚢 Tha Ratchawong pier

END

THA RATCHAWONG PIER
⊞ C6 🚢 Chao Phraya tourist boat to Sathorn pier 🚊 Skytrain Saphan Taksin

1 From Ratchawong pier, walk along Thanon Ratchawong and then turn left onto Thanon Annuwong. To the right is an old Chinese house. Walk on as far as Thanon Maha Chak.

8 Follow the road as far as the fountain on the square, then turn left onto Thanon Traimit to find Wat Traimit (▷ 56) on the left.

2 Take a right here and walk for 160 yards (150m) until you see an ornate portal on the left leading to Wat Chakrawat, where you can visit the crocodile pond.

7 Returning to Soi 16, continue through another exotic food market, which ends in Chinese funerary shops. At the end of the street, turn right onto Thanon Phlabphlachi, with shops selling red and gold shrines. Turn left on Thanon Charoen Krung (New Road).

3 Return to Thanon Maha Chak and turn left, continuing as far as busy Soi Wanit 1 (Sampeng Lane). Turn right here and cross over Thanon Ratchawong.

6 Cross the road and continue about 30 yards (27m) to the left, past fruit and sweet stalls, to the entrance of the Chinese temple of Leng Noi Yee. The temple is very popular with locals, who make all kinds of offerings.

4 Carry straight on, exploring the alleys but always returning to Sampeng Lane as it is easy to get lost. At No. 360, turn left into Soi 16, with its variety of food products.

5 Cross Thanon Yaowarat and walk to Thanon Charoen Krung.

Shopping

ANITA THAI SILK

anitasilk.com

Anita Thai Silk is recommended by expatriates as the place to find reasonably priced and good-quality silk. You'll find a wide selection of fabrics, clothes, bags and soft furnishings.

E7 ⊠ 298/2 Thanon Silom ☎ 0 2234 2481 Skytrain Sala Daeng

ASIA BOOKS

asiabooks.com

This is Thailand's premier bookstore, with a great selection of English-language books and books on all areas of Thailand. There are several branches all over the city.

E7 ⊠ 3rd floor, Thaniya Plaza Building on Thanon Thaniya, off Thanon Silom ☎ 0 2231 2106-7 Skytrain Sala Daeng Silom

ASIATIQUE RIVERFRONT

asiatiquethailand.com

On the site of the old East Asiatic pier, the Asiatique is a sprawling complex of shops and restaurants. You could spend hours browsing the stores and night market for clothes, handicrafts, bags and homewares, have something to eat, take a ride on the Ferris wheel and finish up with a show.

C9 ⊠ 2194 Charoen Krung, Wat Prayakrai, Bangkor Laem ☎ 0 2108 4488 Skytrain Saphan Taksin then free shuttle

BANGKOK FASHION OUTLET

bangkokfashionoutlet.com

Despite its name, this is the place to go if you wish to buy uncut gemstones, although there are a number of outlets to check out, including familiar British names like Marks & Spencer.

E8 ⊠ Jewelry Trade Center, Silom & Surasak intersection ☎ 0 2631 1000 Skytrain Surasak

THE FINE ARTS

A beautiful store selling miniature wooden boats, amulets,19th-century silks and costumes. Also for sale are textiles from Southeast Asia, collected by the owner.

D7 ⊠ Rooms 452–4, River City Shopping Complex, Charoen Krung ☎ 0 2237 0077, ext. 354/452/554 Skytrain Saphan Taksin Tha Sathorn then free shuttle

H GALLERY

hgallerybkk.com

Trend-setting contemporary Thai art can be bought at this gallery in a beautiful old house. Check out the exhibition space.

E7 ⊠ 201 Sathorn Soi 12 ☎ 085 021 5508 Skytrain Chong Nonsi

HEJ STREET BEAUTY

A vision in pink and black, this is the go-to place for fashionable make-up, with many brands exclusive to Thailand. Shoppers are encouraged to try out the products and the prices are good, too.

E7 ⊠ 56 Thanon Silom ☎ 0 2163 6451 Skytrain Sala Daeng

TAILOR-MADE CLOTHES

Bangkok tailors, mostly Thais of Indian origin, have taken over from their Hong Kong brothers. It is cheaper to have a suit made than to buy a designer suit, but remember that you get what you pay for. Some tailors offer a package of two suits, jacket, kimono and shirts, all made in 24 hours for about 4,500B, but the quality will be nonexistent. Choose a tailor with a good reputation, choose a quality fabric and good cut and allow the tailor as much time as possible. You will need to go to the shop to choose your fabric, but fittings can usually be done in your hotel room.

JIM THOMPSON'S THAI SILK COMPANY

jimthompson.com

This is the best, but not the cheapest, place to buy silks and silk clothing. Good, if expensive, silk shirts and neckties are on sale, in a wide, if conservative range of patterns and colors, as well as jackets, pajamas and robes. The company also sells excellent furnishing fabrics, both cotton and silk. There are branches of this store in some five-star hotels and at the Emporium Shopping Complex (▷ 84).

🔼 E7 ✉ 9 Thanon Surawong ☎ 0 2632 8100 🚇 Skytrain Sala Daeng

JOHNY'S GEMS

johnysgems.com

Johny's Gems is one of the city's oldest family-run jewelry emporiums. Choose from a wide selection of jewelry to suit all budgets.

🔼 D6 ✉ 199 Thanon Fueng Nakorn, Chinatown ☎ 0 2224 4065

LAMBERT INDUSTRIES LTD

lambertgems.com

Lambert Industries has been offering gem-cutting services, ready-to-wear jewelry and gemstones for almost four decades, and has an excellent reputation. They make bespoke creations for clients all across the world.

🔼 E7 ✉ 807–809 Silom Shanghai Building, 4th Floor, Soi 17, Silom Road ☎ 0 2236 4343 🚇 Skytrain Surasak

LIN SILVERCRAFT

linjewelers.com

Specialties of this silver shop include cuff links engraved to order, silver necklaces, bangles and cutlery. It is not the least expensive shop in town but the quality is good.

🔼 D7 ✉ 9 Thanon Charoen Krung ☎ 0 2234 2819 🚇 Skytrain Saphan Taksin

LOFT

loftbangkok.com

Browse stationery, homeware and laptop and cell phone accessories, bags, purses and rucksacks at this branch of the stylish chain.

🔼 E6 ✉ Siam Discovery (4th–5th Floor), 989 Rama 1 Road ☎ 0 2658 0328 🚇 Skytrain Sala Daeng

OLD SIAM PLAZA

This might be an old-style shopping plaza, but it is popular with the locals so is really buzzing and loud—and great for picking up some bargain clothing, including silk items. Stop in the food hall for tasty traditional snacks.

🔼 C6 ✉ Thanon Triphet ☎ 0 2226 0156 🚇 Skytrain National Stadium then taxi

PATPONG NIGHT BAZAAR

Bangkok's famous red-light area is also the site for a very popular night market. The sidewalks of Patpong 1 and nearby Thanon Silom fill with stands displaying clothes with counterfeit designer labels,

---

THAI ANTIQUES

Fakes are particularly well made in Thailand and are sometimes sold as genuine antiques. To protect yourself, buy from a reputable shop. Antiques and Buddha images cannot be exported without a license, which can be obtained from the Fine Arts Department at the National Museum (Thanon Naphratad, tel 0 2221 4817). Some antiques stores will arrange the paperwork for you. Applications, submitted with two photographs of the object and a photocopy of your passport, usually take about five days to be processed.

counterfeit Rolex watches, bootleg music and movies, leatherware and other merchandise.

🔲 E7 ✉ Patpong 1 🕐 Nightly 6pm–late 🚇 Silom 🚊 Skytrain Sala Daeng

RIVER CITY SHOPPING COMPLEX

rivercitybangkok.com

This four-story mall overlooks the Chao Phraya River. It specializes in antiques and collectibles but also offers a good selection of fashion outlets as well as riverside restaurants.

🔲 D7 ✉ Charoen Krung Soi 30 (next to Royal Orchid Sheraton Hotel) ☎ 0 2237 0077 🚊 Skytrain Saphan Taksin 🚢 Tha Saphorn then free shuttle

SAMPENG LANE MARKET

A visit to Chinatown is not complete without joining the fray and working your way down the craziness that is Sampeng Lane. Here you can buy pretty much anything. Not only are the narrow lanes jammed with people, but scooters and carts squeeze through as well!

🔲 D6 ✉ Soi Wanit 1 🚇 Hua Lamphong then taxi

SIAM BRONZE FACTORY

siambronze.com

Siam Bronze specializes in quality bronze and stainless steel products. Its trademark is cutlery, dining utensils and homeware, and it will ship worldwide.

🔲 D8 ✉ 1250 Charoen Krung, Bang Rak ☎ 0 2237 1534 🕐 Call for appointment 🚊 Skytrain Saphan Taksin

SILOM VILLAGE

silomvillage.co.th

Silom Village is a popular place for shopping and dining on Thanon Silom. There is a series of several shopping malls, a hotel, spa, the Ruen Thep Thai Dance Center and restaurants. The outlets mostly sell handicrafts and jewelry, but there's also a clothes boutique, luggage shops and a tailor. Prices are quite steep so you need to bargain.

🔲 E7 ✉ 286 Thanon Silom ☎ 0 2234 4448 🚊 Skytrain Chong Nonsi

THAI HOME INDUSTRIES

bangkokriver.com

Shelves heave with baskets, cotton farmers' clothes, temple bells, pretty glass lamps, and settings of the company's stylish, bronze and other metal cutlery at this shop set in a dusty teak house.

🔲 D7 ✉ 35 Charoen Krung, Soi 40 ☎ 0 2234 1736 🚢 Tha Oriental pier

UNIVERSAL TAILORS

Tailors are ten a penny in Bangkok, but this long-established one stands out for the workmanship—this is not the place to go if you want a suit in 24 hours, as work of this quality cannot be rushed.

🔲 E7 ✉ 252/2 Silom Road, Bangrak ☎ 0 81611 2313 🚊 Skytrain Chong Nonsi

THAI SILK

The tradition of silk-making goes back hundreds of years in Thailand, but by the early 20th century Thais preferred less expensive imported fabrics and the industry went into decline. Old skills were being lost when Jim Thompson (▷ 72) discovered a few silk-weavers near his house. Jim Thompson's Thai Silk Company Ltd was founded in 1948 and was well reviewed in *Vogue*. Two years later he was commissioned to make the costumes for the Broadway production of *The King and I* and his success was assured. Jim Thompson's is still the premium purveyor of silk products in Bangkok (▷ 62).

Entertainment and Nightlife

BAMBOO BAR

mandarinoriental.com/bangkok

A Bangkok institution, this stylish bar has a barman who knows how to handle his shaker. After 9pm there are live jazz bands, often from the US. Smart dress is mandatory.

🔲 D7 ✉ Mandarin Oriental Hotel, 48 Soi Oriental ☎ 0 2659 9000 🕐 Sun–Thu 5pm–12.30am, Fri–Sat 5pm–1.30am 🚉 Skytrain Saphan Taksin 🛳 Tha Oriental

BANGKOK SCREENING ROOM

bkksr.com

The first alternative cinema in the city shows independent films, movie classics and documentaries rather than the big blockbusters. There's great digital projection and surround sound, but with just one screen and a mere 52 seats, reservations are essential.

🔲 F7 ✉ 1/3-7 Sala Daeng Soi 1, Silom ☎ 0 90906 3888 🕐 Tue–Fri 3.30pm–midnight, Sat–Sun 11am–midnight 🚉 Skytrain Sala Daeng 🚇 Lumphini, Silom

BANYAN TREE SPA

banyantreespa.com

Enjoy the fantastic views over the city from the 21st floor as you relax in this elegant spa. Massages come in all kinds: Chinese, Balinese and traditional Thai. Spa weekends for couples are on offer.

🔲 F7 ✉ Thai Wah II Building, 21/100 Thanon South Sathorn ☎ 0 2679 1052 🕐 Daily 10-10 🚉 Skytrain Sala Daeng 🚇 Lumphini

CRAFT

The world has gone craft beer mad and Bangkok is no different. Selling a range of mainly American (but some Thai) beers, the staff can help you with your selection. Hearty burgers and pizzas are available to accompany your drink. There's another branch at Sukhumvit 23.

🔲 F7 ✉ 981 Thanon Silom, Khwaeng Silom, Khet Bank Rak ☎ 0 2630 3998 🕐 Daily noon–2am 🚉 Skytrain Surasak

CUBE NIGHTCLUB

The Cube is indeed a boxy club on the second floor of the Silom Plaza, where local, edgy DJs, with some international guest appearances, blast out house and electronic sounds. Saturday night is techno night.

🔲 E7 ✉ Silom Plaza 491, 20 Silom ☎ 0 95252 8301 🕐 Fri–Sat 11pm–late 🚉 Skytrain Chong Nonsi

DISTIL & SKY BAR

lebua.com/distil

The lounge and cigar bar on the 64th floor of the State Tower offers spectacular views and luxurious nibbles. This bar has been used as a movie location in *The Hangover II*.

🔲 D7 ✉ State Tower, 1055 Thanon Silom ☎ 0 2624 9555 🕐 Daily 6pm–1am 🚉 Saphan Taksin

JOE LOUIS PUPPET THEATRE

joelouistheatre.com

Come here to see the disappearing art of the traditional Hun Lakorn Lek Thai puppet theater.

🔲 D7 ✉ Asiatique The Riverfront, 2194 Thanon Charoen Krung Road ☎ 0 2688 3322/0909 🕐 Shows Tue–Sun at 7.30 🚉 Skytrain Saphan Taksin

ADMISSION CHARGES

Many clubs have a cover charge, which usually includes one or two drinks. These charges are often doubled on Friday and Saturday evenings (which are the most exciting nights). Many clubs refuse entry to men in shorts and sandals and prefer smart-casual dress.

KITE-FLYING

Kite-flying is a national pastime in Thailand and can be a serious affair. In Lumphini Park and Sanam Luang, however, the emphasis is on fun. Vendors sell ingenious kites in both parks.

🔡 F7, B–C5 ✉ Lumphini Park and Sanam Luang 🕐 Feb–Apr daily, daytime 🚇 Silom or Lumphini (Lumphini Park) 🚉 Sala Daeng (Lumphini Park); Phaya Thai then taxi (Sanam Luang) 🚢 Tha Chang (Sanam Luang)

MOON BAR

banyantree.com

Perched on the roof of the Banyan Tree Hotel, this sky bar has superb views over the city. The chic open-air lounge is a wonderful spot for an aperitif at sunset before dinner at the adjacent Vertigo grill. Reserve ahead.

🔡 F7 ✉ Banyan Tree Hotel, 21/100 Thanon South Sathorn ☎ 0 2679 1200 🕐 Daily 5pm–1am (weather permitting) 🚉 Skytrain Chong Nonsi 🚇 Lumphini

MUAY THAI LIVE

muaythailive.com

This is the place to experience Thai boxing without the bloodshed. The Legend Lives is an exhilarating theatrical extravaganza about Muay Thai, followed by a couple of rounds of boxing.

🔡 C9 ✉ Asiatique Waterfront, 2194 Warehouse 4, Charoen Krung ☎ 0 2108 5999 🕐 Tue–Sun 8pm 🚉 Skytrain Saphan Taksin then free shuttle

SALA CHALERMKRUNG ROYAL THEATER

salachalermkrung.com

This theater, in a lovely 1930s art deco former cinema, is the perfect place to see *khon* (traditional Thai masked dance drama). English subtitles help foreigners follow the rather complex plots.

🔡 D6 ✉ 66 Thanon Charoen Krung, near crossroads with Thanon Tripetch ☎ 0 2224 4499 🕐 Performances Thu, Fri at 7.30 🚇 Hua Lamphong

THE STRANGER BAR

This small, friendly gay bar in the heart of Silom is one to seek out. It offers a great selection of cocktails, but what really makes it stand out is the nightly drag show.

🔡 E7 ✉ 114/14 Silom 4 ☎ 0 2632 9425 🕐 Daily 5.30pm–2am 🚉 Sala Daeng

TAWANDANG GERMAN BREWERY

tawandang.com

This is a true beer hall with a Thai twist. Enjoy hearty Thai-German food, dance in the aisles to Thai cabaret and drink huge steins of the signature beers. Reservations are essential.

🔡 F9 ✉ 462/61 Thanon Rama III, Khwaeng Chong Nonsi ☎ 0 2678 1114 🕐 Daily 5pm–1am 🚉 Skytrain Chong Nonsi then taxi

THREE SIXTY

hilton.com

It's a grown-up crowd that's drawn to this stylish 32nd-floor bar in the Hilton. The setting is futuristic, the jazz world class and the ambience seductive.

🔡 C7 ✉ Millennium Hilton Hotel, 123 Thanon Charoen Nakorn ☎ 0 2442 2062 🕐 Daily 5pm–1am 🚉 Saphan Taksin then hotel courtesy boat

WHISGARS

whisgars.com

Whisgars offers whiskeys of all kinds in a stylish, relaxed setting. There's live entertainment on Friday nights as well as an unmissable weekly street magic show.

🔡 E7 ✉ 981 Thanon Silom, Bang Rak ☎ 0 2630 1997 🕐 Daily 2pm–2am 🚉 Skytrain Surasak

Where to Eat

PRICES

Prices are approximate, based on a 3-course meal for one person.

$$$ more than 2,000B
$$ 1,000B–2,000B
$ under 1,000B

ARNO'S ($$–$$$)

arnosgroup.com

The waiting list for this steak house, run by French butcher Arnaud Carre and his two Thai partners, has made it one of the hottest spots in town. You order your meat from the counter and tell the chef how you would like it cooked.

🔶 F7 ✉ 2090/2 Soi Naradhiwas 20 ☎ 0 2678 8340 🕐 Daily 11.30–11.30 🚇 Skytrain Chong Nonsi

AUBERGINE ($$)

aubergine.in.th

Trademark French dishes are served in this attractive house on a quiet *soi* off Silom Road. The lamb rack is a favorite, the atmosphere is a blend of classy and cozy and the wine list is impressive.

🔶 E7 ✉ 71/1 Sala Daeng Soi 1/1 ☎ 0 2234 2226 🕐 Daily 11.30am–2.30pm, 6pm–11.30pm 🚇 Sala Daeng

BAAN KHANITHA ($$)

baan-khanitha.com

This huge, popular restaurant has a garden area and is a perfect introduction to Thai cuisine, as the dishes here are adapted to the Western palate.

🔶 E8 ✉ 69 South Sathorn Road. Also at Asiatique ☎ 0 2675 4200 🕐 Lunch, dinner 🚇 Lumphini

BLUE ELEPHANT ($$$)

blueelephant.com/bangkok

The Blue Elephant made its name outside Thailand as a chain of gourmet Thai restaurants. The restaurant and cooking school is in a gorgeous colonial building. The menu offers a good mix of traditional royal cuisine, "Forgotten Recipes" and innovative Thai dishes.

🔶 E8 ✉ Blue Elephant Building, 233 South Sathorn Road ☎ 0 2673 9353 🕐 Daily 11.30am–2.30pm, 6-10.30 🚇 Skytrain Surasak

CELADON ($$–$$$)

sukhothai.com

One of Bangkok's most celebrated and beautiful restaurants is minimalist Thai inside, while outside there are lotus ponds and banana trees. The modern cuisine is just as wonderful; the roast duck curry is particularly good.

🔶 F7 ✉ Sukhothai Hotel, 13/3 South Sathorn Road ☎ 0 2344 8888 🕐 Lunch, dinner 🚇 Skytrain Sala Daeng

EAT ME ($$)

eatmerestaurant.com

Eat Me is an exciting restaurant set over several floors with terraces. The look is modern Asian, the music is great, waiters are friendly and the food is excellent. The menu changes but favorites remain, such as crab and pomelo salad, linguine with spicy soft shell crab and sticky date pudding with hot butterscotch.

CHINESE CUISINE

If you want to cool your palate down after the often fiery Thai food, try one of the Chinese restaurants. Most Chinese in Bangkok come from the Guangdong and Yunnan provinces, well known for their delicious cuisine. The best food can be sampled at the hundreds of inexpensive street stalls in Chinatown, or in the more expensive Chinese restaurants in hotels—there are very few Chinese restaurants in the middle price range.

⊞ E7–F7 ⊠ Soi Pipat 2, off Thanon Convent, Silom ☎ 0 2238 0931 ⏱ 3pm–1am 🚈 Skytrain Sala Daeng

HARMONIQUE ($–$$)

In an old Chinese shophouse filled with antiques and fountains—and a banyan tree—Harmonique is popular for its excellent Thai dishes.
⊞ D7 ⊠ 22 Soi Charoen Krung 34 ☎ 0 2630 6270 ⏱ Mon–Sat 11am–10pm 🚢 Tha Oriental

HORIZON RIVER CRUISE ($$)

shangri-la.com/bangkok
These regular night cruises on the Chao Phraya include an international buffet with fresh salads, broiled fish, meats and very good desserts.
⊞ D7 ⊠ Shangri-La Hotel, 89 Soi Wat Sun Plu, Bang Rak ☎ 0 2236 7777 🚈 Skytrain Saphan Taksin 🚢 Tha Shangri-La pier

LORD JIM ($$$)

This is a superb and incredibly swish fish and seafood restaurant in an elegant setting overlooking the river. It stands out for its impeccable service and the tiny but wonderful little treats between courses, like a smoking sorbet or a pretty amuse-bouche.
⊞ D7 ⊠ Top floor of Mandarin Oriental Hotel, 48 Soi Oriental ☎ 0 2659 9000 ⏱ Lunch, dinner 🚈 Skytrain Saphan Taksin 🚢 Tha Oriental

LOY NAVA ($$–$$$)

loynava.com
Dinner is served on this enchanting teak rice barge full of charm and history. Elegant Thai dancers and musicians add to the atmosphere.
⊞ D7 ⊠ Tha Oriental pier ☎ 0 2437 7329/4932 ⏱ Departs 6pm and 8pm 🚢 Tha Oriental

MANGO TREE ($$)

exquisitethai.com
A charming courtyard setting, attentive service and a superb menu of Thai favorites and delicacies make this a popular choice with locals and tourists. Reservations are advised on weekends.
⊞ E7 ⊠ 37 Soi Tantawan, Thanon Surawongse ☎ 0 2236 2820 ⏱ Daily 11am–midnight 🚈 Chong Nonsi

MEI JIANG ($$$)

peninsula.com
Superb Cantonese dishes are served at this stunning art deco Chinese restaurant with great views.
⊞ D7 ⊠ Peninsula Hotel, 333 Thanon Charoen Nakorn ☎ 0 2861 2888 ⏱ Lunch, dinner 🚈 Skytrain Saphan Taksin (shuttle boat to hotel)

NAHM ($$$)

comohotels.com/metropolitanbangkok
Nahm delivers complex and authentic Thai delicacies in a dining room of chic elegance and sophistication. Standout dishes feature rare ingredients from across Thailand, including a jungle curry with *plu chorn* (a Thai freshwater fish) as well as salty and sweet Thai desserts.

VEGETARIAN OPTIONS

Vegetarians who are visiting Bangkok during the annual Vegetarian Festival (September to October) will find Chinatown awash with food stalls serving Thai and Chinese vegetarian dishes. At other times of the year a choice of fresh vegetable dishes is offered at most Indian and Thai restaurants. Most dishes can be made vegetarian, just mention you are *tann jay*. The city's best vegetarian restaurant is The Whole Earth (⊠ 93/3 Soi Lang Suan, off Thanon Ploenchit ☎ 0 2252 5574).

➕ F7 ✉ Metropolitan Hotel, 27 South Sathorn Road ☎ 0 2625 3388 🕐 Lunch, dinner 🚇 Skytrain Chong Nonsi 🚇 Lumphini

NEVER ENDING SUMMER ($$)

Located in a converted industrial warehouse on the Chao Phraya River, this is a sophisticated spot draped in hanging plants and serving a mix of traditional and more unusual Thai dishes with European influences.

➕ D7 ✉ The Jam Factory, 41/5 Charoen Nakhon Road ☎ 0 2861 0953 🕐 Daily lunch, dinner 🚇 Skytrain Saphan Taksin then Millennium Hotel shuttle boat

LE NORMANDIE ($$$)

mandarinoriental.com

For a formal, elegant dining experience, come to Le Normandie (you'll need to make a reservation). You'll find a choice of exquisite contemporary French dishes prepared by Michelin-starred chefs, impeccable service and stunning views through the full-length windows.

➕ D7 ✉ Top floor, Mandarin Oriental Hotel, 48 Soi Oriental ☎ 0 2659 9000 🕐 Mon–Sat 12–2, 7–10 🚇 Skytrain Saphan Taksin 🚢 Tha Oriental

RUEN URAI ($$)

Don't be put off by the crowds around the notorious Patpong district. This delightful eatery is tucked away in a century-old manor house where the emphasis is on traditional Thai tastes.

➕ E7 ✉ 118 Thanon Surawongse ☎ 0 2266 8268 🕐 Daily noon–11pm 🚇 Skytrain Chong Nonsi

SALA RIM NAAM

mandarinoriental.com

The Mandarin Oriental's Thai restaurant is in a teak house beside the Chao Phraya River and offers a set-menu dinner accompanied by classical Thai dancing. Elegant attire is a must.

➕ D7 ✉ Mandarin Oriental, 48 Soi Oriental ☎ 0 2437 6211 🕐 Dinner from 7pm, dance from 7.45pm 🚇 Saphan Taksin 🚢 Tha Oriental

SALATHIP ($$$)

shangri-la.com/bangkok

Come here for delightful Royal Thai cuisine in the elegant setting of a carved teak pavilion looking out over the Chao Phraya River.

➕ D7 ✉ Shangri-La Hotel, 8 Soi Wat Suan Phu ☎ 0 2236 7777 🕐 Daily 6.30pm–10.30pm 🚇 Skytrain Saphan Taksin 🚢 Tha Oriental or Shangri-La

SILOM VILLAGE ($$)

silomvillage.co.th

Choose from a selection of fresh seafood and other Thai dishes at this huge semi-outdoor restaurant surrounded by craft and textile stores. There is traditional Thai dancing every night while you eat.

➕ E7 ✉ 286 Thanon Silom ☎ 0 2234 4448 🕐 Daily 11–11; dance shows at 8.15 🚇 Skytrain Chong Nonsi

A TYPICAL THAI MEAL

Since the majority of Thais eat at street food stalls or at home, Thai restaurants in Bangkok are more oriented toward foreign visitors who may be unused to chilies. If you want your food red hot, mention it when you order otherwise you will be disappointed. A meal may consist of some appetizers or a spicy salad followed by at least one curry, a noodle dish, steamed rice and a soup. Thais eat with a spoon (right hand) and a fork (left hand). They take just one mouthful of a dish on their plate, then move to the next dish.

Dusit, Siam Square and Sukhumvit

This is the modern part of town, where shopping malls try to outdo each other. But amid the shopping frenzy are some reminders of Bangkok's past, in the old wooden houses set in tranquil gardens.

Top 25

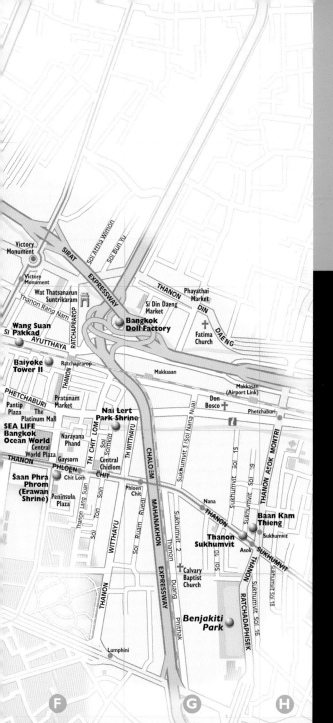

Victory
Monument

Victory
Monument

SIRAT EXPRESSWAY

Soi Attha Wimon

Soi Bun Yu

THANON

Phayathai
Market

DIN DAENG

Si Din Daeng
Market

Wat Thatsanarun
Suntrikaram

Thanon Rang Nam

Bangkok
Doll Factory

Fatima
Church

Wang Suan
Si Pakkad

AYUTTHAYA

Baiyoke
Tower II

Ratchaprarop

Thanon

RATCHAPRAROP

Makkasan

Makkasan
(Airport Link)

Don
Bosco

Phetchaburi

PHETCHABURI

Pratunam
Market

Pantip
Plaza

The
Platinum Mall

Nai Lert
Park Shrine

Sukhumvit 3 (Soi Nana Nua)

THANON ASOK MONTRI

SEA LIFE
Bangkok
Ocean World

Narayana
Phand

TH CHIT LOM

Soi
Somkid

Central
World Plaza

THANON

Gaysorn

PHLOEN

Central
Chidlom

Soi 15

Soi 13

Soi 11

Soi 9

Soi 7

Saan Phra
Phrom
(Erawan
Shrine)

Chit Lom

CHIT

Phloen
Chit

Peninsula
Plaza

Thanon Lang Suan

Soi Ton Son

Soi Ruam Rudi

WITTHAYU

THANON

TH WITTHAYU

CHALOEM

MAHANAKHON

Phloen
Chit

Nana

THANON

SUKHUMVIT

Baan Kam
Thieng

Thanon
Sukhumvit

Sukhumvit

Asok

THANON RATCHADAPHISEK

Sukhumvit Soi 18

Sukhumvit 16

Sukhumvit 10

Calvary
Baptist
Church

EXPRESSWAY

Sukhumvit 2

Thanon
Duang
Phithak

Benjakiti
Park

Lumphini

F

G

H

Baan Jim Thompson

HIGHLIGHTS

● Teak Ayutthaya
architecture
● Exotic landscaped garden
● Views over the *khlong*
● Asian art collection
● Traditional Thai paintings

HIGHLIGHTS

● Teak Ayutthaya
architecture
● Exotic landscaped garden
● Views over the *khlong*
● Asian art collection
● Traditional Thai paintings

TIP

● The canal community
behind the house was
home to many silk
weavers employed by
Jim Thompson and is worth
a quick detour.

**Offering a fascinating introduction to
traditional Thai architecture, a sense of
tranquility away from Siam Square and
an insight into the life of an enigmatic,
mysterious man, Jim Thompson's house
is a Bangkok gem.**

The lost adventurer American architect Jim
Thompson first came to Thailand during World
War II. As he couldn't get used to his uneventful
life back in New York after the war, he decided
to make Thailand his home. Thai culture and
crafts fascinated him, but the day he discovered
some silk weavers near his house his fortune
was secured. He was already something of a
legend when, in 1967, he disappeared during
an afternoon walk in the Cameron Highlands in
Malaysia, never to be seen again. Thompson's

Clockwise from far left: The stairway and checkered tiled hall; Chinese doors leading to a bedroom; the house is set in lush gardens; the house is filled with Thompson's Southeast Asian art and sculpture, like this Buddha figure

friend, the author William Warren, wrote a great account of his life and death, *Jim Thompson: The Legendary American of Thailand,* published in 1970.

Thai-style residence Thompson bought six traditional teak houses in northern and central Thailand, and had them reassembled in Bangkok as his residence, adding Western elements such as stairways and marble floors. The exterior walls were turned inside out to face the interior, and the garden was lovingly landscaped, creating the effect of an oasis. Kept as Thompson left it, the house makes an ideal setting for his small display of Asian art. The collection of traditional Thai paintings is one of the world's best and there are some rare Buddha images.

THE BASICS

jimthompsonhouse. com

⊞ E5

✉ 6 Soi Kasem San 2, off Thanon Rama I, Siam Square

☎ 0 2216 7368

🕐 Daily 9–6

🍽 Small café

🚇 Skytrain National Stadium

♿ None

💷 Moderate (guided tours only)

Baan Kam Thieng

TOP 25

Kam Thieng House is set among formal gardens and trees

THE BASICS

siam-society.org

➕ G6

✉ 131 Soi Sukhumvit 21 (Soi Asoke)

☎ 0 2661 6470

🕐 Tue–Sat 9–5

🍴 Drinks in cafeteria

🚊 Skytrain Asoke

Ⓜ Sukhumvit

♿ Moderate

♿ None

❓ The Siam Society has a library, gallery and small office selling its books. For lectures, check the website

HIGHLIGHTS

● Siam Society Library
● Floral lintels above the door to the inner room to ward off evil spirits

Kam Thieng House is a traditional 19th-century teak stilt house from Chiang Mai. Its collection focuses on the rural lifestyle of northern Thailand.

Lanna Living Museum Unlike Jim Thompson's House (▷ 72) and the Suan Pakkad Palace (▷ 79), Baan Kam Thieng shows how ordinary people lived. It represents a complete northern Thai house with living quarters, kitchen, well, granary, rice pounder, spirit house and household objects and utensils used in everyday life. Farming tools and fish traps are displayed at street level, while upstairs rooms capture the rural lifestyle of 160 years ago. The house was built by the granddaughter of a northern prince, and it is believed that her spirit and those of her mother and granddaughter still inhabit the house: There are many stories of inexplicable incidents occurring here.

Saengaroon House Saengaroon House, originally from Ayutthaya, contains the craft collection of the Thai architect Saengaroon Ratagasikorn, who studied in the US under Frank Lloyd Wright.

Siam Society The lovely garden belongs to the Siam Society, which also has an excellent library, recommended for anyone interested in Thai culture (call before visiting). The society also supports a gallery, holds lectures and publishes books on Thai culture and nature as well as the *Journal of the Siam Society*.

Window detail (left); the mansion is beautifully lit at night (right)

Phra Thi Nang Vimanmek

A tour through Vimanmek Palace, the world's largest golden teak mansion, and the landscaped gardens, gives an insight into the interests of the Thai royal family.

"The Palace in the Clouds" The three-story mansion was originally built in 1868 as a summer house on the island of Ko Si Chang. It was moved wholesale to Dusit in 1901 and reassembled. It soon became King Rama V's favorite palace and was used as the royal residence between 1902 and 1906. It was closed down in 1935 and remained in this state until Queen Sirikit organized its renovation and opened it in 1982 as a museum to mark Bangkok's bicentennial celebrations.

First bathroom Although European influence is clearly visible in the style, Vimanmek is built according to Thai traditions, using golden teak wood and not a single nail. Teak wood contains a special oil that makes it resistant to heat and heavy rains, and which also acts as an insect repellent. Among the possessions of Rama V on display is Thailand's first indoor bathroom and the oldest typewriter with Thai characters, as well as Thai ceramics, china and portraits.

Carriages and crafts The Royal Carriage Museum contains several carriages, mostly imported from Europe, which were popular at the time of King Rama V. The small Suan Farang Kunsai Mansion has oil paintings and photographs of Rama V and his family.

THE BASICS

+ D4
* 193/2 Thanon Ratchawithi
* 0 2228 6300
* Daily 9.30–4.30 (ticket booth 9–3.15)
* Cafeteria on grounds and Thai restaurant near craft shop
* Tha Thewet
* Moderate; free with entrance ticket for Grand Palace (▷ 24–25)

HIGHLIGHTS

● Garden and pond
● Ivory objects in the library

TIPS

● Visitors wearing shorts, miniskirts, flip-flops or sleeveless shirts may not be admitted.
● Free hour-long guided tours are compulsory (in English, every half hour).

Saan Phra Phrom (Erawan Shrine)

Surrounded by fashionable stores, the Erawan Shrine is something of a surprise. Yet the traditional ways of praying and making offerings blend in perfectly with the new and modern city culture.

Spirit house The Erawan Shrine was erected as a spirit house connected to the Erawan Hotel, which has now made way for the Grand Hyatt Erawan Hotel. The construction of the original hotel in 1956 was beset with problems, including cost overruns and injuries to workers, so spirit doctors advised that a shrine be built with a four-headed image of Brahma (Phra Phrom in Thai). After that, work progressed smoothly and the shrine became famous for bringing good fortune. Erawan is the Thai name for Brahma's three-headed elephant.

From left: Worshipers laying offerings at the shrine; classical Thai dancers wearing traditional costume perform at Saan Phra Phrom

Merit-making Right on a busy sidewalk, the shrine is often a scene of chaotic activity. People come here to offer colorful flower garlands, lotus flowers, incense and candles; after a few minutes at the shrine your senses tend to go into overdrive. Often, if a wish has been granted, people thank the spirits by donating teak elephants or commissioning the classical dancers and live orchestra to perform. Outside the shrine, women sell birds in tiny cages, which are believed to bring good fortune and earn merit if you set them free. The variety of worshipers here is also surprising: older people, Thai families with children, and fashionable younger women in the latest Western designer clothes all kneel down to perform the same traditional rites. The walkway from Chit Lom station offers good views from above.

THE BASICS

- F6
- Corner of Thanon Ratchadamri and Thanon Phloen Chit
- Early morning to late night
- Restaurants nearby
- Skytrain Chit Lom or Ratchadamri
- Good
- Free

Thanon Sukhumvit

TOP 25

Benchasiri Park is a welcome green space on busy Sukhumvit Road

Sukhumvit Road runs like a major artery through the heart of Bangkok. The area is a buzzy, lively and fun part of the city to explore.

Getting around The area has welcomed the arrival of some extremely high-end luxury and boutique hotels. The many *soi* that branch off Sukhumvit are home to hotels, restaurants and bars, tailors and trendy nightclubs, as well as catering to those in search of Bangkok's more infamous forms of entertainment.

Shopping galore The seemingly endless street of Sukhumvit, and the *soi* off it, have all the shopping in the world. (The area is served by the safe and cheap Skytrain so you can avoid the traffic.) Around Soi 11 are several crafts shops with good tourist items. Soi 23 has some better crafts shops with Thai produce. The huge Emporium Shopping Complex combines Western and Thai designer stores (▷ 84), while H.M. Factory for Thai Silk (▷ 84–85) on Soi 39 is good for ties, scarves and accessories. Thong Lor or Soi 55 remains noted for its cool bars and restaurants.

Entertainment Much of the city's nightlife now happens in the *soi* off Sukhumvit Road. Some of the most on-trend bar-clubs are on Soi 8, 11 and Soi Siam Square 6, including Chi Ultralounge (▷ 88) and Det-5 (▷ 88–89). For a different atmosphere head for Little Arabia around Soi 3 and Soi 5.

Wang Suan Pakkad

Tropical gardens surround the buildings (below, right); detail of dancers (middle)

Suan Pakkad Palace is a lovely corner amid urban sprawl. Like Jim Thompson (▷ 72), its owners were passionate and discerning collectors of Thai arts and traditional architecture.

"Cabbage Farm Palace" Prince and Princess Chumbhot of Nakhon Sawan moved these eight traditional Thai houses from Chiang Mai (some had belonged to the prince's great-grandfather) in 1952. The cabbage garden was turned into one of Bangkok's finest landscaped gardens and is calm in a uniquely Eastern way. The princess was one of the country's most dedicated art collectors, and the house has been turned into a museum displaying every-day objects such as perfume bottles and musical instruments. Antiques include an exquisite Buddha head from Ayutthaya, Khmer statues and European prints of old Siam.

Ban Chieng House An entire house is devoted to the elegant pottery and bronze jewelry discovered at Ban Chiang, an important Bronze Age settlement in northern Thailand, dating from around 1600–500BC.

Lacquer Pavilion The exquisite Lacquer Pavilion, once part of an Ayutthaya monastery, was moved here in 1959. The gold and black lacquer murals depict events from the life of the Buddha and the *Ramakien*, the Thai version of the *Ramayana* epic. The lower layer is notable for its representations of daily life.

THE BASICS

⊞ F5
✉ Thanon Sri Ayutthaya
☎ 0 2245 4934
🕐 Daily 9–4
🍴 Restaurants around Victory Monument
🚈 Skytrain Phaya Thai
♿ None
✋ Moderate

HIGHLIGHTS

● Lacquer Pavilion
● Buddha head from Ayutthaya
● Lovely enclosed garden
● Wonderful prints of old Siam by European artists

More to See

BAIYOKE TOWER II

baiyokeskyhotel.com

No longer the city's tallest building (that is now MahaNakhon in Silom), Baiyoke Tower II is still a good place in this part of town for sweeping views over Bangkok. A hotel occupies the 22nd to 50th floors and there are observation decks on the 77th and 84th floors. Go on a clear day. The glass elevator shoots up a corner of the building, and is not recommended for anyone nervous of heights.

🔲 F5 ✉ Thanon Ratchaprarop, Prathunam ☎ 0 2656 3000 🕙 Daily 10.30–10.30 💵 Moderate 🚉 Skytrain Phaya Thai

BANGKOK DOLL FACTORY

bangkokdolls.com

Come here to see Khunying Tongkorn Chandevimol's private collection of dolls from her own factory and all over the world. Family members make the fine Thai dolls, inspired by Thai history and mythology, which are now sold all over the country.

🔲 F5 ✉ Soi Ratchataphan (Soi Mo Leng), off Thanon Ratchaprarop ☎ 0 2245 4532 🕙 Tue–Sat 8.30–5 🚉 Skytrain Victory Monument, then taxi 💵 Free

BENJAKITI PARK

This much-needed 52-acre (21ha) green zone opened in celebration of Queen Sirikit's Sixth Cycle (72nd birthday). Work continues to expand the park with the planting of indigenous flora.

🔲 G7 ✉ Thanon Ratchadaphisek 🕙 Daily 5am–8pm 🚉 Sirikit Center

CHURCH OF THE IMMACULATE CONCEPTION

In 1567, Portuguese traders brought Christianity to the old capital of Ayutthaya, and soon afterward, the first Christian missionaries also arrived. The French Catholic missionaries, who arrived much later in 1662, had a greater influence on the Catholic Church in Bangkok itself, but it was the Portuguese who founded one of the city's earliest churches, the

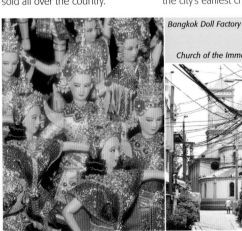

Bangkok Doll Factory

Church of the Immaculate Conception

lovely white Immaculate Conception Church in Samsen. The original church was built in 1674 during the reign of King Narai, but the present church dates from 1847. On the compound there is a smaller, older church known as Wat Noi, now used as a museum for religious relics.

🔲 C3 ✉ 167 Soi Mitrakam Samsen, off Soi 11 Thanon Samsen, Dusit ☎ 0 2243 2617, ext.167 ⏰ Daily 8am–4pm, church 6–8pm 🎫 Free 🚢 Tha Thewet

MUSEUM OF FLORAL CULTURE

Housed within a century-old home and gardens, this museum from the highly regarded Thai floral designer Sakul Intakul looks at the importance attached to flowers and their use in religious and royal ceremonial occasions, as well as in everyday Thai life.

🔲 D3 ✉ Samsen Soi 28 off Nakorn Chasi ☎ 0 2669 3633 ⏰ Tue–Sun 10–6 🎫 Inexpensive 🚉 Skytrain Saphan Taksin then take the Orange Flag Chao Phraya Express Boat to Payap pier

NAI LERT PARK SHRINE

In the back garden of the stylish Nai Lert Hotel, next to the *khlong*, is a rather unusual lingam shrine. Several phalluses carved in stone or wood surround the spirit house built by millionaire businessman Nae Loet in honor of the female deity, who is thought to inhabit the old sacred banyan tree on that spot. The shrine is incredibly popular with young women as it is believed to help fertility.

🔲 F5 ✉ Swissotel, Nai Lert Park Hotel, 2 Thanon Witthayu 🎫 Free 🚉 Skytrain Phloen Chit

ROYAL THAI ELEPHANT MUSEUM

Alongside Vimanmek Palace (▷ 75), the two stables that once provided a home for the royal white elephants now make up a museum devoted to the role of elephants in Thailand's history and society, with displays of equipment and information. The importance of white elephants is explained: the animals

Museum of Floral Culture

The Royal Thai Elephant Museum

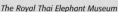

are albinos (more brown than white) whose rarity made them sacred and the property of the king. When a white elephant was spotted, and its authenticity accredited by experts, an elaborate ceremony accompanied its presentation to the king. Photographs of the proceedings are on show in the museum.
🔲 D4 ✉ Thanon Ratchawithi ☎ 0 2228 6300 🕐 Daily 9.30–4 🍴 Restaurants at Dusit Zoo 🚉 Phaya Thai then taxi 🚤 Tha Thewet 💷 Price included in entry to Vimanmek Palace (▷ 75)

SEA LIFE BANGKOK OCEAN WORLD

sealifebangkok.com

Take an enthralling journey through the habitats of the southern oceans at this attraction, and encounter the weird and wonderful flora and fish that live in the sea. The sharks can be seen being fed twice a day.
🔲 F6 ✉ B1-B2 Floor, Siam Paragon, 991 Thanon Rama I, Pathumwan
☎ 0 2687 2000 🕐 Daily 10–9
💷 Expensive 🚉 Skytrain Siam

SIAM PARK CITY

siamparkcity.com

It's a little out of the city but this amusement and water park will thrill children. It's popular with locals too so best visited on weekdays. Tickets can be reserved online. Height restrictions apply for certain rides.
🔲 Off map ✉ 203 Suan Siam Road, Kannayao ☎ 0 2919 7200 🕐 Daily 10–6
💷 Moderate 🚕 Best reached by taxi from your hotel

WAT BENCHAMABOPHIT

The "Marble Temple" is built from Carrara marble in a blend of traditional Thai temple architecture and European designs. There is a collection of 53 Buddha images in the courtyard. It is a perfect place to watch religious festivals and moonlit processions. The monks don't go out seeking alms but are visited by merit-makers between 6 and 7am.
🔲 D4 ✉ Corner of Thanon Si Ayutthaya and Thanon Rama V ☎ 0 2282 7413
🕐 Daily 6–6 🍴 Foodstalls 💷 Inexpensive

A fretwork bridge spanning a pond at Wat Benchamabophit

Prathunum

Discover an interesting mix of buildings, old and new, where the slick urban lifestyle is never far from traditional rural ways.

DISTANCE: 2–2.5 miles (3.5–4km) **ALLOW:** 1.5 hours

START

NATIONAL STADIUM
🚇 E6 🚉 Skytrain National Stadium

END

SUAN PAKKAD PALACE
🚇 F5 🚉 Skytrain Phaya Thai

❶ Follow Thanon Rama I to the west and note the National Stadium on your left, Thailand's main football stadium, with an art deco facade.

❷ Cross Thanon Rama I and turn right into the narrow lane of Soi Kasem San II, with Jim Thompson's House (▷ 72) at the end. Retrace your steps down Soi Kasem and turn left on Thanon Rama I.

❸ The Mahboonkrong Center, popular with teenagers and with a good food hall (▷ 85), is on the right. Cross Thanon Phaya Thai, and ahead lies the lively Siam Square.

❹ Return to Thanon Phaya Thai, and turn left. Walk to Chulalongkorn University, with an interesting mix of buildings set in a beautiful garden with a lake and an art gallery.

❽ Back on Thanon Ratchaprarop, walk left on Thanon Sri Ayutthaya past Suan Pakkad Palace (▷ 79). Head to Phaya Thai Skytrain station.

❼ Walk up Thanon Ratchadamri, across Thanon Phetburi, and find to the left Prathunum market on Thanon Ratchaprarop, with food stands, tailors and clothing shops. Back on Thanon Ratchaprarop, walk left and take the first street to the left to find the Baiyoke Tower II (▷ 80).

❻ Turn right on Rama I again and find, on the junction, the Erawan Shrine (▷ 76).

❺ Walk out on Henri Dunant Road, turn left and go to the end of the road.

Shopping

ALMETA
almeta.com
Almeta specializes in weaving to order and monogramming bed linens. You can buy Thai silks in hundreds of shades and weights here, as well as sumptuous silk wallpaper.
🕂 H6 ✉ 20/3 Sukhumvit Soi 23 ☎ 0 2204 1413 🚇 Skytrain Asoke 🚇 Sukhumvit

L'ARCADIA
L'Arcadia is a small store with well-priced antique furniture and carved teak architectural ornaments, mainly from Thailand and Myanmar (Burma).
🕂 H6 ✉ 12/2 Soi Sukhumvit 23 ☎ 0 2259 9595 🚇 Skytrain Asoke 🚇 Sukhumvit

EMPORIUM SHOPPING COMPLEX
emporium.co.th
This huge shopping center is the place to come for all the designer brands of the moment, including Prada, MiuMiu, Shanghai Tang and Louis Vuitton, plus less expensive labels such as Jaspal and Stefanel. There is an amazing food hall on the fifth floor and a large fresh fruit and vegetables area where you can buy exotic Thai fruits and fresh herbs. Counters sell ready-made Thai desserts and delectable snacks.
🕂 H7 ✉ Soi Sukhumvit 24 🚇 Skytrain Phrom Phong

EXOTHIQUE THAI
A huge selection of Thai crafts is available at Exothique, which has a contemporary vibe. This is a great place to stock up on celadon plates, organic spa products with Thai herbs, relaxing Thai cushions as well as ethnic-inspired silk clothing.
🕂 H7 ✉ 4th floor, Siam Paragon ☎ 0 2664 8000, ext. 1554 🚇 Skytrain Phrom Phong

GAYSORN PLAZA
gaysorn.com
An exclusive shopping center that is all about glittering marble floors, top designer labels and an incredibly well-heeled clientele.
🕂 F6 ✉ Corner of Thanon Ploenchit and Thanon Ratchadormi 🚇 Skytrain Chit Lom

GOOD SHEPHERD
goodshepherdbangkok.com
The Good Shepherd's Fatima Shop has a wide range of handicrafts and embroidery for sale from producer groups and crafts people across Thailand. The money received goes to support the Good Shepherd Sisters ministries and helps to improve the lives of people and families whose work is sold.
🕂 H7 ✉ 591/17 Sukhumvit Soi 22 ☎ 0 2245 0457 🚇 Skytrain Phrom Phong

GREYHOUND
greyhound.co.th
Greyhound sells chic and contemporary casual wear for men and women plus a more edgy collection, called Playhound by Greyhound, for younger people.
🕂 F6 ✉ Siam Center, and branches on Rama I ☎ 0 2251 4917 🚇 Skytrain Siam

HERRMANN FASHIONS
herrmannsuits.com
Herrmann Fashions has been trading on the same premises for almost a quarter of a century. Custom-made tailoring is the stock in trade but it's also a good place if you want to buy Thai silk.
🕂 G6 ✉ 73/1 Sukhumvit, Soi 3 ☎ 081 844 7768 🚇 Skytrain Nana

H.M. FACTORY FOR THAI SILK
hmfactory-thaisilk.com
Mr. Pipat Vanijvongse built a small silk factory and a showroom in his house in

1957 and it's still going strong. As well as purchasing scarves, ties, cushions and accessories made from the finest Thai silk, customers can also see the manufacturing process at work.

J8 45 Soi Promchai, Sukhumvit Soi 39 0 2258 8766 Skytrain Phrom Phong

KINOKUNIYA

Bangkok's largest and best English bookstore sells a wide range of both locally printed and imported books.

H7 3rd floor, EmQuartier Shopping Complex, 689 Sukhumvit Road 0 2003 6507 Skytrain Phrom Phong

KNOT

knot-designs.com

In the market for a new watch? Then head to Knot—a branch of the Japanese watchmaker that lets customers customize their own watch, selecting the dial, case, strap and buckle from the Japanese-made range.

H7 Sukhumvut Soi 47 0 2258 4877 Phrom Phong

MAHBOONKRONG (MBK) CENTER

mbk-center.co.th

You can buy everything from knockoff designer labels to cell phone accessories at this shopping mall (particularly lively on weekends). Stores range from teenage favorites to the more upscale Tokyu department store. There is a good food court here too.

E6 Corner of Thanon Rama I and Thanon Phaya Thai Skytrain National Stadium or Siam Square

NARAI PHAND

naraiphand.com

This huge crafts and souvenir emporium usually offers good value.

F6 973 Ploenchit Road 0 6560 3989 Skytrain Chit Lom

NARRY TAILOR

narry.com

Voted Bangkok's "Tailor of the Year" for several years running, Narry offers good-quality work and quick service. Phone for a free pick-up.

G6 155/22 Thanon Sukhumvit Soi 11/1, near Swiss Park Hotel 0 818 347 545 Skytrain Nana

PANTIP PLAZA

Pantip Plaza is another huge shopping mall with seven floors dedicated to technology—computer hardware, software, pirated versions of everything and all the latest gadgets.

F5 Petchaburi Road, opposite Pratunam's City Complex Skytrain Chit Lom, then take a taxi or walk

PAPAYA

This vast warehouse is filled with some of the most stylish furniture from the past 100 years. It's hard to find but well worth the trouble. Walk up Thanon Ratchadamri and leave Gaysorn Plaza to

SHOPPING MALLS

Bangkok shopping malls rival those you would find in any major international city. Designer brands and multinational names tend to dominate but it is still possible to find the occasional specialist or boutique retailer. These malls also have food halls, upscale dining options, multiplex cinemas, spas and much more. The largest and most swish of these are Siam Paragon (▷ 86, siamparagon.co.th), Emporium (▷ 84, emporium.co.th), MBK Center (▷ 85, mbk-center.co.th) and Siam Center (siam-center.co.th).

your right. Go under the second pedestrian walkway and turn right at the Citizen Building. Continue until you find Seefah Restaurant; Papaya is on the opposite side of the road, up the steep ramp.

🏠 F5 ✉ 89/57 Bangkok Bazaar, Thanon Ratchadamri ☎ 0 2655 3355 🚇 Skytrain Chit Lom

PIRUN THONG

Looking for some different furnishings to add a touch of Thai style to your home? This shop offers a range of pillows, curtains, throws and lamp shades ready made or produced to order.

🏠 J8 ✉ Sukhumvit Soi 45–47 ☎ 0 2258 7296 🚇 Skytrain Phrom Phong

PRAYER TEXTILE GALLERY

prayertextilegallery.com

You can buy old and new traditional textiles from northern Thailand, Laos and Cambodia at this gallery, as well as some ready-made garments.

🏠 E6 ✉ Phaya Thai Road, Siam Square ☎ 0 2251 7549 🚇 Skytrain Siam

PROPAGANDA

propagandaonline.com

A bright and cheerful place in the Emporium Shopping Complex (▷ 84), Propaganda sells funky designs with a humorous twist. Look out for the shark bottle opener, the plastic homeware and bright T-shirts.

🏠 F5 ✉ 4th Floor, Emporium Shopping Complex ☎ 0 2658 0430 🚇 Skytrain Siam

REFILL STATION

Like almost everywhere else in the world, Bangkok is looking to curb waste. This green business—started by three friends—is the first bulk store in Thailand where you can bring empty containers

of shampoo, shower gel and detergent to refill. The store stocks eco-friendly products such as bamboo toothbrushes and also hosts recycling workshops. There's a café on site too.

🏠 K8 ✉ Sukhumvit Soi 77/1 ☎ 0 8693 6566 🚇 Skytrain Phra Khanong

ROBINSON

store.robinson.co.th

Robinson's is an institution in Bangkok with several branches around the city, including Sukhumvit. Whatever you need, whether it be underwear, toiletries, gifts or clothes, you can find it here at bargain prices.

🏠 G6 ✉ 259 Sukhumvit, North Klongtoey, Wattana ☎ 0 2252 5121 🚇 Skytrain Asoke or Nana

SIAM PARAGON

siamparagon.co.th

The latest and glitziest of all shopping malls is the Siam Paragon, with all the major international designer labels as well as mainstream brands like Gap, a huge department store, a floor dedicated to Thai crafts and design, and a vast cinema complex.

🏠 F6 ✉ 991 Thanon Rama I, Siam Square ☎ 0 2610 8000 🕐 Daily 10–10 🚇 Skytrain Siam

TAILOR ON TEN

tailoronten.com

It may not be the cheapest tailor in a part of town where there's (at least) one on each corner, but Tailor on Ten has established an international reputation for its in-house tailoring, fine fabrics and designs that reflect both traditional and modern styling. Despite its name, it is actually on Sukhumvit Soi 8.

🏠 G9 ✉ 93 Sukhumvit Soi 8 ☎ 0848 771 543 🚇 Skytrain Nana

Entertainment and Nightlife

THE AUSTRALIA PUB & BBQ

theaustraliabangkok.com

This sports bar and restaurant is one of the places to catch major sporting events televised from around the world.
➕ G6 ✉ Sukhumvit Soi 11 ☎ 0 2651 0800 🕘 Daily 9am–late 🚈 Skytrain Nana

BACCHUS & CO

Bacchus is one of the trendiest places to be seen in Bangkok. It's a multi-level wine bar offering a range of wines and spirits and regular tasting events. The relaxing top floor has a glass ceiling where you can enjoy the night sky.
➕ G6 ✉ Sukhumvit Soi 16 ☎ 0 2258 0259 🕘 Daily 10am–10.30pm 🚈 Skytrain Phloen Chit

BANGKOK OPERA

bangkokopera.com

This company—which presents the best of the international opera repertoire and some home-grown favorites—performs at locations across town, primarily the Thailand Cultural Centre (▷ 89). Visit the website to view the latest schedule.

BREW

brewbkk.com

Bangkok has acquired a taste for fine ales and an interest in the craft beer movement. Brew meets the demand with a staggering 500 varieties of beer and cider in surroundings reminiscent of a Belgian brewery.
➕ G6 ✉ 30 Sukhumvit Soi 11 ☎ 0 2255 5532 🕘 Daily 11am–1am 🚈 Skytrain Asok

BRITISH COUNCIL

britishcouncil.or.th

This is the most active of the foreign cultural centers in Bangkok, and offers regular lectures, movies, concerts, music and dance.
➕ E–F6 ✉ 254 Chulalongkorn Soi 64, Siam Square, off Thanon Phaya Thai ☎ 0 2657 5678 🕘 Daily 9.30am–6pm 🚈 Skytrain Siam Square

CHEAP CHARLIE'S

Bizarre, surreal and certainly unique, this little bar attracts both tourists and locals. The drinks are cheap, the atmosphere lively and the decor boasts oddities (from buffalo skulls to beehives and tribal masks) collected over its 20-year history.
➕ G6 ✉ Sukhumvit Soi 11 (take the first left) ☎ 0 2253 4648 🕘 Mon–Sat 5pm–12.30am 🚈 Skytrain Asok

CHI ULTRALOUNGE

The famed Bed Supperclub has closed, been taken apart and reassembled, retaining its elliptical, spaceship-like structure, one street away to emerge as this new hot spot. Part nightclub, part Asian fusion food eatery and part chilled lounge, it's pretty much business as before.
➕ G6 ✉ Sukhumvit Soi 13 ☎ 0 2662 1936 🕘 Daily 8pm–2am 🚈 Skytrain Nana

DET-5

det-5.com

Noted for its relaxed atmosphere and live music scene, Det-5 is popular with both tourists and the city's expats. It serves food (Thai and international) throughout the day and has an

---

REVITALIZE

Bangkok is wonderful but it can be exhausting. All over the city you'll see small spa shops offering a range of excellent, inexpensive treatments. A heavenly one-hour foot massage will leave you relaxed and ready for another day.

open-mic night on Mondays (from 8.30pm), instruments provided.

🏠 G6 ✉ 41 Sukhumvit Soi 8 ☎ 0 2653 1232 ⏰ Daily 10pm–2am 💵 Admission charge 🚇 Skytrain Nana

GLOW

This boutique bar and club has a reputation for showcasing the best electronic music. The offering changes nightly and the experience is a mix of intimate style, dramatic lighting and funky decor.

🏠 G6 ✉ 96/4–5 Sukhumvit Soi 23 ☎ 0 2261 4446 ⏰ Daily 7pm–late 🚇 Skytrain Asok

THE LIVING ROOM

thelivingroomatbangkok.com

Offering fabulous jazz and an impressive cocktail list, The Living Room mixes comfort with style and is one of the city's most alluring hotel bars. It also offers a Grande Afternoon Tea (Saturday 3–8pm) and is said to have one of Bangkok's best Sunday brunches.

🏠 G6 ✉ Sheraton Grande Sukhumvit, 250 Sukhumvit ☎ 0 2649 8353 🚇 Skytrain Asok

RUEN-NUAD MASSAGE STUDIO

A real find, this long-established massage studio offers excellent Thai or aromatic oil massages.

🏠 H6 ✉ 18/1 Sukhumvit Soi 31 ☎ 0 8123 0888 ⏰ Daily 10.30–9 🚇 Skytrain Asok

SIAM NIRAMIT

siamniramit.com

This show is a spectacular extravaganza with more than 150 performers taking the audience on a journey through Siamese history using state-of-the-art special effects.

🏠 J4 ✉ 19 Thanon Tiamruammit, Huaykwang ☎ 0 2649 9222 ⏰ Daily shows at 8pm 🚇 Thailand Cultural Centre

SOI COWBOY

Elements of Bangkok's nightlife are infamous but for the most part it's all done with humor and you're unlikely to experience much in the way of hassle. Soi Cowboy, a short street with around 40 or so go-go bars, is a good choice if you want to satisfy your curiosity but avoid the more full-on clubs and bars of Nana Plaza and Patpong.

🏠 H6/7 ✉ Sukhumvit between Soi Asoke (Sukhumvit Soi 21) and Sukhumvit Soi 23 ⏰ Daily til late 🚇 Skytrain Asok

SPA 1930

spa1930.com

A full range of massage, spa and beauty treatments is available at this delightful spa. They'll even create one especially to deal with the mental and bodily fatigue of jetlag.

🏠 G6 ✉ 42 Soi Tonson, Lumphini ☎ 0 2254 8606 ⏰ Daily 9.30am–9.30pm; advance reservation recommended 🚇 Skytrain Phloen Chit

THAILAND CULTURAL CENTRE

Come to this modern theater venue for concerts by the Bangkok Symphony Orchestra, as well as drama and classical Thai dance.

🏠 H4 ✉ Thanon Ratchadaphisek, Huai Khwang ☎ 0 2247 0028 ⏰ Thailand Cultural Centre (free bus to center on performance days)

OFF TO THE MOVIES

Thais love going to the movies and Bangkok's cinemas now rival anything you'd find elsewhere in the world when it comes to comfort. International films are screened in English with Thai subtitles. Be respectful and stand for the national anthem. The leading chain is Major Cineplex (majorcineplex.com).

Where to Eat

PRICES
Prices are approximate, based on a 3-course meal for one person.
$$$ more than 2,000B
$$ 1,000B–2,000B
$ under 1,000B

ANA'S GARDEN ($–$$)

Amid skyscrapers, this garden restaurant offers a welcome retreat from the hectic city. The food is traditional Thai.

🔼 J7 ✉ 67 Soi 55 Sukhumvit ☎ 0 2712 8877 🕐 Daily 5am–midnight 🚊 Skytrain Thong Lo

BAN KHUN MAE ($–$$)

bankhunmae.com

Expect straightforward but well-prepared Thai food here. The restaurant is popular with young Thais and families.

🔼 E–F6 ✉ 458/6-9 Siam Square Soi 8, Rama I Road ☎ 0 2658 4112 🕐 11am–10pm 🚊 Skytrain Siam

BASIL ($$$)

basilbangkok.com

This popular Thai restaurant serves excellent traditional cuisine in a contemporary setting. It looks like a beautiful deli, with jars of curries and marinades, and a floor-to-ceiling rack filled with wine from all over the world. Make sure you leave some space for the mouthwatering desserts.

🔼 G6 ✉ Sheraton Grande Sukhumvit, 250 Thanon Sukhumvit ☎ 0 2649 8366 🕐 Daily 12–2.30, 6–10.30, Sun Jazz brunch 12–3 🚊 Skytrain Asok

BO.LAN ($$$)

bolan.co.th

Michelin-starred and a hot reservation, Bo.Lan takes the finest ingredients from sustainable sources across Thailand to create a menu that changes every few months. Courses are dispensed with—food is all served together Thai-style.

🔼 J7 ✉ 24 Sukhumvit Soi 53 ☎ 0 2260 2961 🕐 Tue–Fri 6–10.30, Sat–Sun 12–2.30, 6–10.30 🚊 Skytrain Thong Lo

BOURBON STREET ($$)

bourbonstbkk.com

New Orleans and Southern-style specials such as jambalaya, blackened red fish and pecan pie feature on the menu of this Cajun restaurant, and there is an American-style bar.

🔼 J7 ✉ 9/39-40 Soi Tana Arcade, Sukhumvit 63 ☎ 0 2381 6801 🕐 Daily 7am–1am 🚊 Skytrain Thong Lo

BROCCOLI REVOLUTION ($–$$)

broccolirevolution.com

This modern vegan restaurant and cold-pressed juice bar offers a diverse menu of dishes from all over the region and overseas.

🔼 J7 ✉ 899 Sukhumvit 49 ☎ 0 2662 5001 🕐 Mon–Fri 7am–10pm, Sat–Sun 9am–10pm 🚊 Skytrain Thong Lo

CRÊPES & CO. ($)

crepesand.co

This is Bangkok's favorite crêperie in a beautiful Thai villa set in an exotic garden. The pancakes are delicious, but also on offer is a selection of salads and Mediterranean dishes.

🔼 F6 ✉ 59/4 Soi Langsuan Soi 1 ☎ 0 2015 3388 🕐 Daily 9am–midnight 🚊 Skytrain Chit Lom or Phloen Chit

DOSA KING ($)

dosaking.net

Dosa, thin crêpes made from lentil and rice batter, are the basis for the vegetarian meals served at this inexpensive eatery off Thanon Sukhumvit.

🔢 G6 ✉ 153/7 Sukhumvit Soi 11 ☎ 0 2651 1651/2 🕐 Daily 11–11 🚆 Skytrain Nana

ENOTECA ITALIANA ($$)

enotecabangkok.com

Tucked away in a residential area, Enoteca Italiana could well be one of Bangkok's best-kept culinary secrets. The food is delicious, the wine cellar is hugely impressive—and room must be reserved for the homemade ice creams.

🔢 H7 ✉ 39 Sukhumvut Soi 27 ☎ 0 2258 4386 🕐 Daily 6pm–midnight 🚆 Skytrain Phrom Phong 🚇 Sukhumvit

GOVINDA ($$)

Govinda is a good Italian vegetarian restaurant serving a wide range of salads, pastas and vegetable dishes.

🔢 H7 ✉ 22 Mall Plaza, Sukhumvit Soi 22 ☎ 0 2663 4970 🕐 Daily 6–11pm 🚆 Skytrain Phrom Phong

GREYHOUND CAFÉ ($$)

greyhoundcafe.co.th

Part of the Greyhound fashion house, this cool Western-style eatery offers a global menu including sashimi, salads and Thai dishes.

🔢 J7 ✉ J Avenue, Sukhumvit Soi 55 (or on 2nd floor of the Emporium Shopping Complex, ▷ 84) ☎ 0 2712 6547 🕐 Daily 11am–10pm 🚆 Skytrain Thong Lo

INDUS ($$–$$$)

indusbangkok.com

Indian restaurants in Bangkok can be of variable quality but Indus, with its countless awards, modern interior (lovely garden dining area) and imaginative menu with a lighter, healthier twist, is a bit of a gem.

🔢 H7 ✉ 71 Sukhumvit Soi 26 ☎ 0 2258 4900 🕐 Daily 11.30–2.30, 6–10.30 🚆 Skytrain Phrom Phong

KUPPA ($$)

This trendsetting Australian-managed café, in a casual and spacious interior, is lively and buzzing at any time of the day. The food is a global mix of grills, salads and pastas, but do keep a space for the delicious homemade cakes.

🔢 G-H7 ✉ 39 Sukhumvit Soi 16 ☎ 0 2259 1954 🕐 Daily 10.30am–11.30pm 🚆 Skytrain Asok

THE LOFT

This modern food court, in a black minimalist interior with great lighting, has a plastic card paying system instead of the usual vouchers. Food stands sell Thai and Vietnamese dishes as well as a few classy Western-style desserts, and everything tastes wonderful. It is more expensive than the standard food court on the first floor, but worth it.

🔢 F6 ✉ Central Department Store, Thanon Phloen Chit 🕐 Daily 10–10 🚆 Skytrain Chit Lom

MAHANAGA ($$$)

mahanaga.com

Come here for inventive Thai-fusion cuisine complemented by a superb

FOOD COURTS

Thais love eating their snacks or meals at food courts, usually located around shopping malls or office areas. The atmosphere is great sitting outside at night, while on a hot day the air-conditioned environment is a tempting option. Venues vary from the basic snack-type place found close to supermarkets to fashionable upscale food courts like the stylish Loft in Chit Lom. Food courts are a great way to sample a range of Thai dishes and flavors at small prices. Every stand or mini kitchen has its specialties and ingredients are always fresh.

wine list. The interior decor is Moroccan inspired and there is a small courtyard-style garden. It's great for a romantic night out, but reserve ahead.

⊞ H6 ✉ 2 Sukhumvit Soi 29 ☎ 0 2662 3060 ⏱ Dinner 5.30–11pm, bar open til late 🚇 Skytrain Asoke

NIPPON TEI ($$$)

nippontei.com

Considered to be one of the best Japanese restaurants in town, Nippon Tei offers sashimi and sushi as well as Kobe beef and seafood.

⊞ F6 ✉ 161 Nantawan Bldg, Thanon Ratchadamri ☎ 0 2252 9438 ⏱ Lunch, dinner 🚇 Skytrain Ratchadamri

PEPPINA ($–$$)

peppinabkk.com

Peppina adheres to the rules of the Associazone Verace Pizza Napoletana, an organization created to protect the heritage of genuine Neapolitan pizza. The resulting pizza base is just as it should be—pillowy and soft with a blistered crust.

⊞ H6 ✉ 27/1 Sukhumvit 33 ☎ 0 2119 7677 ⏱ Daily 11.30–2.30, 6–12 🚇 Skytrain Asok or Phrom Pong

RANG MAHAL ($$)

Some of the finest South Indian food in town is served here in pleasant and ele-gant surroundings, and accompanied by Indian classical music.

⊞ H7 ✉ Rooftop of Rembrandt Hotel, 19 Sukhumvit Soi 18 ☎ 0 2261 7100 ⏱ Daily 6–11pm, Sun brunch buffet 11am–2.30pm 🚇 Skytrain Asoke

ROSSINI'S ($$–$$$)

rossinisbangkok.com

Designed in the style of an enchanting Tuscan villa, Rossini's is defined by the passion, creativity and flair of its gifted Sicilian-born chef, Gaetano Palumbo. The jazz brunch on a Sunday is especially popular.

⊞ G6 ✉ Sheraton Grande Sukhumvit, 250 Sukhumvit ☎ 0 2649 8364 ⏱ Mon–Fri, Sun 6.30–10.30am, 12–2.30, 6.30–11pm, Sat 6.30–11am, 6–10.30pm 🚇 Skytrain Asok

RUEN MALLIKA ($$)

ruenmallika.com

It's a bit hard to find, but you are transported to another time when you do locate this converted teak house set in a lush garden. On the menu is excel-lent Thai cuisine, from hot and spicy dishes from the south to traditional curries as served to the royal family.

⊞ H7 ✉ 189 Sukhumvit Soi 22 ☎ 0 2663 3211 ⏱ Daily 11–11 🚇 Skytrain Asoke

VIENTIANE KITCHEN ($$)

vientiane-kitchen.com

This restaurant serves some of the most exciting food in town, mainly from Isaan province and Laos. The flavors are com-plex, intriguing and extremely delicious; really spicy if you want it to be. The ser-vice is peaceful and friendly, making the dining experience utterly pleasing. A live band plays traditional music, and with the open-air atmosphere really makes for a special evening.

⊞ J7 ✉ 8 Naphasap Yak 1, Sukhumvit Soi 36 ☎ 0 2258 6171 ⏱ Daily noon–midnight 🚇 Skytrain Thong Lo

---

MASSAMAN CURRY

Massaman curry, rich and relatively mild, is a staple on the menu of many restaurants in Thailand. Typically made with chicken or beef, and accompanied by potatoes and roasted peanuts, it is served in a delicious aromatic broth.

Farther Afield

If the pace in the city gets to you, head out to the not-exactly-quiet Chatuchak Market, find rural Thailand on Bangkok's *khlongs*, or learn more about the country's history at Ayutthaya or at the River Kwai.

Top 25

Bight of Bangkok
(Ao Krung Thep)

3261

352

3214

305

305

3312

3312

✈ Don Mueang

Safari World

304

351

Siam Park
City

304

Prasart
Museum

3119

7

✈ Suvarnabhumi

3001

7

34

9

3344

7

3268

34

3268

1006

3268

3

3

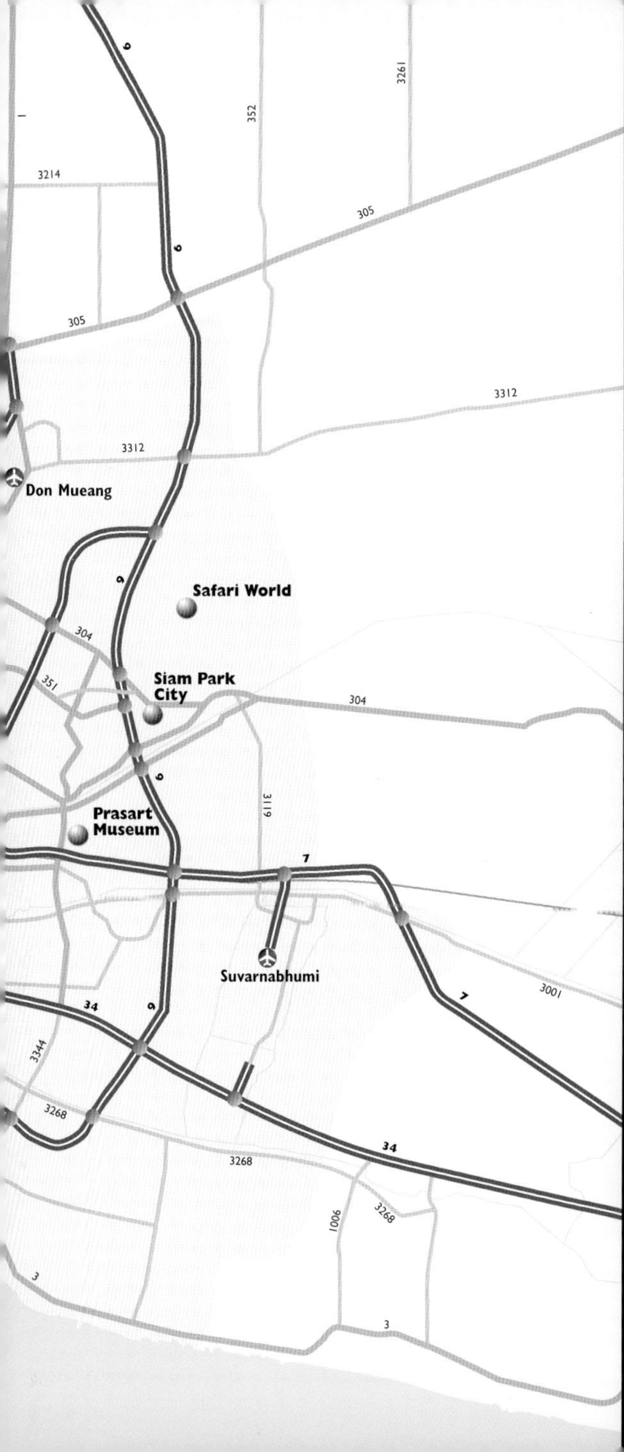

Chang Chui Creative Park

HIGHLIGHTS

● Runway Bar under the Lockheed airplane
● Chui Play zone
● Vintage cinema
● Food stalls
● Coffee bars
● Craft beers at Oldman Café
● Contemporary sculptures such as the giant bronze skull

An actual TriStar Lockheed airplane towers over the gigantic futuristic sculptures, food stalls, amusements and entertainment venues at this innovative cultural park.

Land of infinite creativity Opened in 2017, the park has already made it onto *Time* magazine's list of the world's 100 greatest places. Intended to inspire and excite visitors through new ideas on art—much of it made from reused materials such as empty perfume bottles—design, retail and entertainment, the result is a thriving creative hub and a one-stop destination for everything art-related. The range of street entertainment, amusements, craft collectives, theater and film shows and retail outlets means there is something for everyone.

Clockwise from far left: the TriStar Lockheed is an incongruous sight in Bangkok's cityscape but makes a perfect centerpiece for this offbeat park; the many shops on the site sell all kinds of interesting and unusual items, from stationery to stuffed animals; the giant bronze skull is one of the many art installations dotted around the park

What to see You can happily spend many hours at Chang Chui. Start at the massive retired Lockheed aircraft that sits majestically smack in the middle of the 6.5-acre (2.7ha) site and is the symbol of the park, and a great backdrop for a selfie. You can't go inside but there is a bar underneath, one of more than 100 eateries here serving everything from oysters and pizza to crispy fried insects. Chui Play is a corner of the park with a classic funfair atmosphere, where you can try your hand at shooting games, basketball hoops and more. Finally, in one of the world's finest cities for shopping, Chang Chui makes its own unique contribution. Whether you're a collector of antiques, have an eye for the talent of emerging artists or are a fan of designer labels, you're likely to find something of interest here.

THE BASICS

changchuibangkok.com

➕ A3

✉ 460/8 Sirindhorn Road, Bang Phlat

☎ 0 8181 72888

🕐 Mon–Tue, Thu–Fri 4–11, Sat–Sun 11–11; best visited in the evening

♿ Few

🎟 Free

Chatuchak Weekend Market

HIGHLIGHTS

● Amulets and collectors' items, Section 1
● Antiques, Section 26
● Hill-tribe textiles and crafts, Section 24

TIPS

● When you become footsore, stop at one of the many foot massage stalls.
● Smoking is prohibited in the market.
● More and more vendors are opening up Friday evenings as well.

This weekend market feels like the mother of all markets. Known to locals as J.J., this is a shopping extravaganza where you will find everything you could possibly need on sale.

General view Before going, get hold of Nancy Chandler's *Map of Bangkok* (available from English-language bookstores and online), which has a detailed map of Chatuchak showing what is for sale and where. With 15,000 stalls spread across 35 acres (14ha) attracting around 200,000 visitors every weekend, the market can be daunting; luckily there are dozens of foodstalls to stop at when you need a break.

Everything for sale You could spend a whole day here and not see all of it but, if time is

Visitors to the market can make a day of it—there is so much to see and buy, and if you need refreshments you'll find cafés and food vendors

limited, make sure you arrive early to avoid the worst of the crowds and heat. A lovely way to get to the main market is to get off the Skytrain early at Saphan Khwai and wander through the amulet market first. The market is divided into sections, with handicrafts and souvenirs in sections 1, 25 and 26. Clothing is available right across the market, and the selection of sarongs alone in cotton and silk is bewildering.

Antique caution Sections 1 and 26 are the areas to head to for antiques, although many dealers have now moved to J.J. Plaza, next to the market, which is open daily. Unless you really know your stuff, don't take everything the vendor says at face value or assume that everything you see is antique. Whatever you are buying, make sure you bargain!

THE BASICS

chatuchakmarket.org
⊞ G2
✉ Thanon Phahonyothin, near Chatuchak Park
🕐 Sat–Sun 9–6
🍴 Foodstands and cafés throughout the market
🚇 Skytrain Mo Chit
🚉 Chatuchak Park
♿ None
💲 Free

Khlong Bangkok Yai

HIGHLIGHTS

● Life and boats along
the *khlongs*
● Murals in Wat
Welurachin
● Wat Inthararam's
painted doors
● Amulets from Wat
Pak Nam

TIP

● Arrange with the boat-
man at any of the main
piers to get you a long-tail
boat and to tell the driver
exactly what you want, at
the same price you would
get elsewhere.

**A great way to escape Bangkok's busy
traffic is to take to the water—a ride
on the riverbus or a trip on the canals.
Khlong Bangkok Yai leads from the Chao
Phraya to the treasures of Thonburi.**

From the river For many Bangkok residents,
canals (*khlongs*) remain an important means of
getting around the city and for the visitor they
provide eye-opening views. The easiest and
cheapest way of getting along Khlong Bangkok
Yai is on one of the regular long-tail boats from
either Tien or Rajinee piers on the Chao Phraya.
On the right (north) bank as you enter the
canal lies Wat Sang Krachai, dating from the
Ayutthaya period and restored by early Chakri
kings. As you pass under the first of Thonburi's
main bridges, look for Wat Welurachin on the

Bangkok's canals are important to the city: they are a way of getting around without having to negotiate the busy roads, and many people live along them

left bank, with its 19th-century murals. Beyond the next bridge is Wat Inthararam (left bank), containing the ashes of King Taksin, who moved the Siamese capital to Thonburi in 1768, where he was deposed and killed 14 years later. It has beautiful lacquer decorations inside and out.

Back to the river At the junction of Khlong Sanam Chai and Bangkok Noi sits Wat Pak Nam, a huge temple from the Ayutthaya period, noted for its meditation center. From here Khlong Bangkok Yai curves north to meet Khlong Bang Noi (left) and Khlong Mon (right), which leads back to the Chao Phraya River. Across this junction, Khlong Bangkok Yai is called Khlong Chak Phra and leads to Khlong Bangkok Noi, and then to the Royal Barges Museum (▷ 30) and the Chao Phraya River.

THE BASICS

✚ A7–B7

🍴 Floating foodstalls along the *khlong*

🚢 Regular boats from Tha Chang, Tha Tien, Tha Rajinee and Memorial Bridge piers

Prasart Museum

The traditional teak buildings here are a wonderful introduction to Thai culture

THE BASICS

➕ See map ▷ 95
✉ 9 Soi 4A, Thanon Krungthepkritha, off Thanon Srinakarintora, 97 Bang Kapi
☎ 0 2379 3601/7
🕙 Fri–Sun 10–3
✋ Expensive (includes a guide and a drink)
❓ Take a taxi (20–30 min from Siam Square). Admission by appointment only, so call ahead

HIGHLIGHTS

● Landscaped garden
● Red Palace
● Lanna-style Buddhas
● Benjarong ceramics
● Some visitors are lucky enough to meet Mr. Prasart himself

TIP

● Benjarong ceramics can be bought in the River City Shopping Complex (▷ 63).

It has been property tycoon Khun Prasart Vongsakul's mission to buy Thai antiques and objets d'art that had been sold abroad, and to restore them to Thailand. His museum is now an education and research center.

A private museum This rarely visited but superb collection is housed in an array of traditional Thai buildings, painstakingly reconstructed small temples, teak houses and palaces from all over Asia. The aim was to convey a flavor of the different Asian styles, not to create an exact reproduction. The delightful landscaped garden is home to some stunning Sukhothai-style terracotta pieces, and also has rare Thai and imported plants. This private museum in the Bang Kapi suburb gives a clear introduction to Thai art, architecture and history.

Many pavilions The golden teak Red Palace is an exquisite reproduction of the Tamnak Daeng, built in the Rama III period, now in the National Museum (▷ 29). Stunning antiques from the Ayutthaya and early Rattanakosin periods are found here, including furniture, and ornate gold vessels. The wooden Lanna Pavilion has a beautiful collection of Lanna-period Buddha images and a European-style mansion has period household utensils, beautiful Benjarong ceramics and Western art objects. Other buildings include a teak-wood library set over a lotus pond, a Lopburi-style chapel, a water garden and a Khmer Guanyin Shrine.

More to See

CHILDREN'S DISCOVERY MUSEUM

Set aside a day for kids of all ages for digging for dinosaur bones in the Dinosaur Detective zone, building Lego, splashing around in the water park, scrambling through the Jungle Adventure and joining in creative activities.

➕ See map ▷ 95 ✉ Queen Sirikit Park, Khamphaeng Phet 4, Chatuchak ☎ 0 2272 4500 ⏰ Tue–Sun 10–4 💷 Free 🚇 Skytrain Mo Chit 🚃 Chatuchak Park

MUSEUM OF CONTEMPORARY ART

mocabangkok.com

Spread over five floors of a striking building with lots of natural light, the collection here consists of an eclectic mix of contemporary paintings and sculpture. There are also temporary exhibitions.

➕ See map ▷ 95 ✉ 499 Kamphaeng Phet 6, Ladyao, Chatuchak ☎ 0 2953 1005 ⏰ Tue–Fri 10–5, Sat–Sun 11–6 🍴 Café 💷 Expensive 🚇 Skytrain Mo Chit then taxi 🚃 Phahon Yothin

QUEEN SIRIKIT PARK

This park near Chatuchak Weekend Market (▷ 98) was built to commemorate the 60th birthday of the Queen. A wonderful open space with botanical gardens and colorful tropical birds, the park also has a blind garden with signs in Braille. A pool winds its way through the park and the fountains in it entertain visitors three times a day.

➕ G1–2 ✉ 820 Thanon Phahonyothin ⏰ Daily 5am–6pm 💷 Free 🚇 Skytrain Mo Chit 🚃 Chatuchak Park

SAFARI WORLD

safariworld.com

Thailand's largest zoo includes giraffes, lions and rhinos seen on a drive through the park, plus a marine park and bird area. Visitors can see tigers and lions being fed and get up close to giraffes on a head-height viewing platform.

➕ See map ▷ 95 ✉ 99 Thanon Panyaintra, Samwatawantok, 5 miles (9km) from city center ☎ 0 2518 1000 ⏰ Daily 9–5 💷 Expensive 🚇 Skytrain Mo Chit

Main visitor area, Safari World

Portrait of H.M. Queen Sirikit

Excursions

AYUTTHAYA

When Bangkok was a small village, Ayutthaya was Thailand's capital, a glittering city on an artificial island encircled by canals, with scores of palaces, temples and over a million inhabitants.

Founded around 1350, it was the capital of Siam for more than 400 years, until it was sacked by the Burmese in 1767. The old island city was designated a UNESCO World Heritage Site in 1991. To get an overview of the scattered remains, start off at the Historical Study Center (Thanon Rotchana, tel 0 3524 5124). Don't miss the temples of Wat Mahathat, Wat Ratburana, Viharn Phra Mongkol Bopit and Chantharakasem National Museum.

BANG NAM PHUENG FLOATING MARKET

This weekend market in Phra Pradaeng is easily reached by crossing the Chao Phraya River to an area known as the "green lung of Bangkok."

Most of the stalls are actually by the water rather than on it and the narrow lanes are perfect for a bit of exercise, so consider renting a bike. As a working market, it is popular with Thais searching for local specialties grown in the vicinity. Browse the foodstalls and then sample the freshly cooked food at wooden tables by the water.

BANG PA-IN PALACE

In the mid-19th century at Bang Pa-In, the Thai royal family built a retreat beside the Chao Phraya River. The palace incorporates classical Thai, Chinese and European elements and is surrounded by extensive manicured gardens and lakes—rent a golf cart to tour the site. Modest dress is required. The palace makes a good stop-off on the way to Ayutthaya.

KO KRET

This tiny island in the Chao Phraya River feels a world away from Bangkok, with wooden houses hidden among the palm trees, and is ideal for walking or cycling. It's known for its pottery, *kwan arman*, which is baked, unglazed red clay carved with intricate patterns—buy a coffee on the island and you'll get a little pot as a souvenir. Across the main pier you will see the strangely leaning Wat Paramaiyikawat, with a marble Buddha. There is a popular weekend market here, when the island gets very busy.

THE BASICS

worldcrocodile.com
Distance: 9 miles (15km) north of Bangkok
Journey Time: 20 minutes
🍴 Several riverside restaurants 🚤 Chao Phraya Express boat to Nonthaburi or Pak Kret, then cross-river ferry to Ko Kret

MUANG BORAN

This is a large open-air museum where more than 100 small versions of the most important Thai temples, palaces and traditional houses, some brought in and reconstructed on site, are spread over a Thailand-shaped area. This could be tacky, but is actually well done and makes for a pleasant day out. Heat permitting, the lush tropical gardens are great for cycling (cycle hire is included in the entrance price) and, since this is Thailand, foodstalls and restaurants offer plenty of opportunities for snacks and drink.

THE BASICS

ancientcity.com
Distance: 20 miles (33km) south of Bangkok
Journey Time: 2 hours
✉ 269/1 Sukhumvit Road, Bangpho, Samut Prakan
☎ 0 2323 4094 🕐 Daily 9–7 💰 Expensive
🚈 Skytrain Bearing then taxi

NAKHON PATHOM

This sleepy town is home to Thailand's tallest Buddhist monument, the 394ft (120m) Phra Pathom Chedi. The original was built by sixth-century Buddhists of Dvaravati, but it was abandoned for a long time after the 11th century and the current structure dates from 1870. It is covered in shiny ceramic tiles. Set in alcoves around the base of the chedi are hundreds of representations of the Buddha, and in the *bot* is an Ayutthaya-style Buddha seated in a European pose. The temple is one of the six most sacred temples in the country.

THE BASICS

Distance: 35 miles/56km west of Bangkok
Journey Time: 1 hour
🚌 Daily service from Thonburi's Southern Bus Terminal
🚆 Express train at 8.05am; more in the afternoon from Hua Lamphong station

FARTHER AFIELD EXCURSIONS

THE BASICS

Distance: 79 miles (130km) west of Bangkok
Journey Time: 2–3 hours
🚆 Two trains daily for Kanchanaburi from Bangkok Noi station 🚌 Buses from Bangkok's Southern Bus Terminal, Thonburi (every 20 min until late evening) 🛈 TAT office, Thanon Sangshuto (☎ 03451 1200)

RIVER KWAI

The focus of the movie *The Bridge on the River Kwai*, the Burma Railway (often called the Death Railway) was built for the Japanese forces in Burma by Allied prisoners of war and Asian laborers in World War II, with the loss of many thousands of lives. A tourist train now runs along the tracks. Kanchanaburi, the town near the bridge, is the site of the JEATH War Museum, which contains personal effects of the prisoners and photos showing the brutal conditions under which they lived. Also here is the Kanchanaburi War Cemetery, the last resting place of 6,982 Allied prisoners of war.

THE BASICS

Distance: 18 miles (30km) northeast of Bangkok
Journey Time: 45 mins
✉ 171 Paholyothin Road, Don Mueang Airport ☎ 0 2534 1853 🕐 Daily 8–4 🎫 Free 🚆 Don Mueang station then taxi

ROYAL THAI AIR FORCE MUSEUM

Aviation started in Thailand with demonstration flights during 1911, and later that year, three Thai Army officers were sent to France to train as aviators.

This museum has a great collection of planes, including a Cessna 0-1 Bird Dog, a Douglas Skyraider and a Vought V-935 Corsair, the last one remaining in the world, as well as displays exploring Thailand's role in World War II.

THE BASICS

siamwinery.com
Distance: 31 miles (50km) southwest of Bangkok
Journey Time: 1 hour
✉ 9/2 Moo 3 Tumbon Bangtorud, Mueang, Samut Sakhon ☎ 0 3484 5334 🕐 Mon–Sat tours at 10 and 1 🎫 Expensive 🚌 From Southern Bus Terminal, Bangkok

SIAM WINERY

Southeast Asia's largest vineyard was established in 1986 by Chalerm Yoovidhya.

This is close to floating vineyards where farmers grow the local Malaga Blanc and Red Pokdum grapes under the eyes of an experienced German team of winemakers. The wines have now won several awards and have become recognized internationally. Tours include the vineyard, the wine-making process and wine tasting. The winery also cultivates grapes at its Monsoon Valley Vineyard near Hua Hin, and has its own range of Moose cider.

Where to Stay

It can seem like a new hotel opens in Bangkok every month, making the range one of the most extensive of any world city. Actually choosing one, however, can be a challenge. Our guide gives you the geographical lowdown followed by recommendations across different price ranges.

Introduction

Bangkok is a sprawling metropolis and accommodations are consequently spread across a wide area. The first thing to consider, even before your budget, is where you want to base yourself.

The Choices
If you want to spend a lot of time shopping and dining out and require good transportation connections, then Thanon Sukhumvit and the *soi* that run off it are worth considering. Budget-wise, this is a mid-range area but it also has some top-class hotels like the Four Seasons as well as good budget places. For luxury, you need to stay by the river or, for chic places like the Met and the Sukhothai, along the top end of Thanon Sathorn Tai. Banglamphu and the Thanon Khao San area are good for budget accommodations, but there are also good mid-range places here and the area is convenient for the Grand Palace and Dusit.

What to Expect
Rates at all the hotels vary according to demand and time of year, falling during the rainy season and escalating in the high season, rising even higher if there is a big festival or event in town. Apart from at quality hotels, it is normal practice to be shown your room before you agree to stay. In budget places you should check the shower and hot water and door locks, and if appropriate the availability of mosquito nets and how well the windows close. Nonsmoking rooms are more common now, but do check.

OUT OF THE ORDINARY

Many hotels in Bangkok are large multinationals, but the city still has plenty of more characterful places. Bangkok Tree House (bangkoktreehouse.com) is a calming oasis with impressive green credentials; Old Bangkok Inn (old-bangkokinn.com) is pretty much (and impressively) what it says on the label; and Ariyasom Villa (ariyasom.com), built in the early 1940s and still run by the same family, is a small boutique hotel just off Sukhumvit.

Stay in a traditional teak house or plush new hotel—you're sure of a warm welcome

Budget Hotels

ATLANTA

theatlantahotel.bangkok.com

Atlanta is a popular, old-fashioned 1950s hotel on central Sukhumvit with simply decorated, air-conditioned or fan-cooled rooms and a swimming pool. The hotel has a reputation for friendly service and appeals to families.

➕ G6 ✉ 78 Soi Sukhumvit 2 ☎ 0 2252 6069 🚇 Skytrain Phloen Chit

BANGKOK CHRISTIAN GUESTHOUSE

bcgh.org

This is a lovely Christian-based guest-house with wonderful staff, 57 simple but very tidy rooms and a great, lush lawn with a fish pond.

➕ F7 ✉ 123 Soi Sala Daeng 2, off Thanon Convent, Silom ☎ 0 2233 6303 🚇 Skytrain Sala Daeng

BOONSIRI PLACE

boonsiriplace.com

Close to the Grand Palace and Wat Pho, the 48 rooms here boast contemporary Thai decor, each room decorated with different oil paintings depicting various cultural styles.

➕ C5 ✉ 55 Buranasart Road, Pranakorn ☎ 0 2622 2189 ⛴ Tha Chang

FURAMA XCLUSIVE SUKHUMVIT

furama.com

Location is the selling point here, with nightlife, shopping and a Skytrain stop right on hand. It's all wrapped up in a stylish boutique hotel setting.

➕ G6 ✉ 27 Sukhumvit Soi 1 ☎ 0 2255 4244 🚇 Skytrain Phloen Chit

RIVER VIEW GUEST HOUSE

riverviewbkk.com

This place has spacious rooms overlooking the Chao Phraya. A good breakfast of cereal and fresh fruit is served on the top floor.

➕ D7 ✉ 768 Soi Phanurangsri, Songwad Road, Talad Noi ☎ 0 2234 5429 🚇 Hua Lamphong

SHANTI LODGE

shantilodge.com

A quiet hotel set in a garden, the Shanti Lodge has well-kept and air-conditioned rooms, all decorated in Thai style.

➕ C4 ✉ 37 Sri Ayudhya Road, Soi 16 (behind National Library) ☎ 0 2281 2497 ⛴ Tha Thewet

TRINITY SILOM

trinitysilomhotel.com

Offering contemporary accommodations in an ideal downtown location, Trinity Silom is well presented and the rooms (and other facilities) are of a good standard for the price. It's within the Trinity Complex so guests may make use of the extensive leisure facilities.

➕ E7 ✉ 150 Silom Soi 3 ☎ 0 2231 5050 🚇 Skytrain Chong Nonsi

THANON KHAO SAN

First came backpackers in search of the pleasures of the Orient, then local Thais and Chinese who saw the possibilities. Thanon Khao San and its neighborhood is now the place for cheap beds, low-cost eats, low-cost clothes and low-cost beer. If you're on a tight budget, this is the place to be, but arrive early in the day if you want to find a bed. One thing's for sure, it's going to be lively. Thanon Khao San is also popular with young Thais as the place to go for a beer in the evening.

Mid-Range Hotels

BEL-AIRE

belairebangkok.com

The Bel-Aire offers affordable luxury just a stone's throw from the hustle and bustle of Thanon Sukhumvit and a five-minute walk from the Skytrain. There's a bar, lounge, restaurant and pool.

➕ G6 ✉ 16 Sukhumvit, Soi 5 ☎ 0 2253 4300 🚉 Skytrain Nana

BUDDY LODGE

buddylodge.com

The smartest hotel in the street, this boutique hotel offers comfortable rooms decorated with Thai designs and incorporating a lot of wood. The very laid-back atmosphere is in tune with the backpackers' haven outside.

➕ C5 ✉ 265 Thanon Khao San ☎ 0 2629 4777 🚤 Tha Phra Athit

CHANN BANGKOK NOI

channbangkoknoi.com

Tricky to find (but that's part of the charm), this urban retreat in a historic part of the city is full of character. Based around two teak-wood houses linked by wooden walkways, the design inside is contemporary, with substantial use of wood and natural fabrics. The 22 rooms and suites are spread across two floors. It's best reached by taxi.

➕ B5 ✉ 30/1 Wat Dusitaram Somdej, Phra Pin Klao Road ☎ 0 2435 5997 🚤 Prachan cross-river ferry pier

DREAM

dreambkk.com

An ultra-modern hotel where sleep is taken seriously in its 195 rooms as they are all lit by ethereal, sleep-inducing blue lights. The hotel also features a rooftop pool, restaurant and spa.

➕ G6 ✉ Soi Sukhumvit 15 ☎ 0 2254 8500 🚉 Skytrain Nana

GRAND CHINA PRINCESS

grandchina.com

If you want to stay in Chinatown then this is the hotel to choose. The 155 rooms have all the necessary amenities and the hotel has a choice of places to eat, including a revolving restaurant at the top. There's also music in the lobby at night, a fitness center and a Thai massage service.

➕ D6 ✉ 215 Thanon Yaowarat ☎ 0 2224 9977 🚉 Hua Lamphong 🚤 Tha Ratchawongse

HIP BANGKOK

hip-bangkok.com

Decorated in a colorful contemporary style, this is a good-value choice if a central location isn't important—although it is close to a Metro station. Facilities include private karaoke rooms if you don't fancy going out for your entertainment.

➕ H3 ✉ 111/1 Soi Niam U-tit Ratchadaphisek Road, Dindaeng ☎ 0 2276 5777 🚉 Huai Khwang

IBRIK RESORT HOTEL ON THE RIVER

ibrikresort.com

This small three-room boutique hotel has a rare riverfront location with views of the Grand Palace. The very stylish rooms all have air-conditioning, a bathroom and balcony.

➕ B5 ✉ 256 Soi Wat Rakang, off Thanon Arunamrin, Bangkok-noi ☎ 0 6008 5589 🚤 Cross-river ferry from Tha Chang to Tha Wat Rakang or Tha Wang Lang

JIM'S LODGE

jimslodge.com

A quiet, pleasant hotel located within easy walking distance of a choice of restaurants, Lumphini Park and shops, Jim's Lodge offers 75 rooms, all with air-conditioning, satellite TV and private bathrooms.

➕ G6 ✉ 125/7 Soi Ruam Rudee, off Thanon Ploenchit Lumphini ☎ 0 2255 3100 🚇 Skytrain Phloen Chit

LUXX

staywithluxx.com

One of two Luxx hotels in Bangkok—the other can be found in Langsuan—this small boutique hotel with just 13 rooms is close to the shopping, restaurant and nightlife scene of Silom. The design is contemporary and chic and the bathrooms all have a signature wooden bathtub.

➕ E7 ✉ 6/11 Decho Road, Bangruk ☎ 0 2635 8800 🚇 Skytrain Silom and Chong Nonsi

MUSE

hotelmusebangkok.com

This modern and stylish hotel is on the relatively quiet Langsuan Road, just a short walk from the Skytrain. Even the standard rooms here push the boundaries in comfort and lovely furnishings while the 19th-floor infinity pool and rooftop bar all add to the appeal.

➕ F6 ✉ 55/555 Langsuan Road, Lumphini, Pathumwan ☎ 0 2630 4000 🚇 Skytrain Chit Lom

LA RÉSIDENCE

laresidencebangkok.com

This is a small boutique hotel located above the All Gaengs restaurant (curries are their specialty) on Surawong. La Résidence has 26 lovely rooms with cable TV, air-conditioning and minibar.

➕ E7 ✉ 173/8–9 Thanon Surawong ☎ 0 2233 3301 🚇 Skytrain Chong Nonsi

RIVA ARUN

rivaarunbkk.com

It's the show-stealing rooftop bar and restaurant with majestic views (especially at night) across the river to Wat Arun and Wat Pho that make this something of a gem. The interior decor here is all modern, clean lines with tasteful artworks and enticing communal areas. The studio rooms are a little on the compact side.

➕ B5 ✉ 392/25–28 Maharaj Road ☎ 0 2221 1188 ⛴ Tha Tien

THE SIAM HERITAGE

thesiamheritage.com

Close to both the Skytrain and the Metro, this charming boutique hotel is in an excellent location. The 73 rooms and suites reflect traditional Thai style with polished wooden floors and antique teak furniture complemented by Thai silk accents. Amenities include a Thai restaurant, rooftop swimming pool and spa.

➕ E7 ✉ 115/1 Surawong Road, Bangrak ☎ 0 2353 6166 🚇 Skytrain Sala Daeng 🚇 Samyan

A RANGE OF HOTELS

You get what you pay for in the top end and budget categories of accommodations, but in the mid-range things are less clear. The lobby usually looks good but the rooms may not be of the same standard. You may also find that there is a coming and going of massage girls or call girls during the night. The hotels mentioned on these pages all have some character, are clean, and prefer guests to go up to their room alone.

Luxury Hotels

137 PILLARS SUITES & RESIDENCES

137pillarsbangkok.com

One of the newest luxury offerings on Sukhumvit Road, 137 Pillars is both stylish and indulgent. The owners have taken their inspiration partly from an old property they bought in Chiang Mai, which boasted 137 pillars (the number of pillars was seen as a mark of wealth and importance).

J7 ☒ Sukhumvit Soi 39 ☎ 0 2079 7000 ⊛ Skytrain Phrom Phong

BANYAN TREE

banyantree.com

One of the tallest hotels in town, with an excellent spa, the Banyan Tree's views from the rooftop and the 62nd-floor restaurant are stupendous. All 216 rooms are equipped with the latest office gadgets, and there's a pool.

F7 ☒ 21/100 South Sathorn Road ☎ 0 2679 1200 ⊛ Skytrain Sala Daeng ⊛ Lumphini

CAPELLA

capellahotels.com

The latest of Bangkok's high-end hotels, Capella is an all-suite and villa property. Ultra-sleek design, an iconic riverside location and a Michelin-starred chef are the key attractions.

C6 ☒ 39 Charoen Krung Road ☒ Tha Tien

FOUR SEASONS BANGKOK

fourseasons.com/bangkok

An impressive modern hotel in the heart of Bangkok with a grand, old-style atmosphere, imposing lobby, shopping arcade and 354 lovely, elegant rooms.

F6 ☒ 155 Ratchadamri Road ☎ 0 2126 8866 ⊛ Skytrain Ratchadamri

LOY LA LANG

loylalang.com

For those who prefer small luxurious hotels rather than large international ones, this seven-room teak house is a haven right on the Chao Phraya River in the peaceful grounds of Wat Pathumkongka.

D6 ☒ 1620/2 Songwat Road, Sampanthawong ☎ 0 2639 1390 ⊛ Hua Lamphong ☒ Tha Ratchawongse

MANDARIN ORIENTAL

The Mandarin Oriental is a Bangkok institution (▷ 58).

PENINSULA

peninsula.com/bangkok

The famous Peninsula hotel is considered to be one of the best in the world. There are 370 fully equipped rooms, all with excellent views of the river and large, sumptuous marble bathrooms with TVs. The restaurants are excellent, and there is a three-tiered swimming pool in the garden. The service is superb.

D7 ☒ 333 Thanon Chareon Nakorn ☎ 0 2861 2888 ⊛ Skytrain Saphan Taksin, then free shuttle boat ☒ Free shuttle boats from Oriental, River City and Shangri-La piers

Need to Know

Use this section to help you plan your visit to Bangkok. We have suggested the best ways to get around the city and useful information for when you are there.

Planning Ahead

When to Go

The most pleasant time to visit, and the peak tourist season, is from November to early March, so flights and lodgings are best reserved ahead. During the hot season, invest in an air-conditioned room. In the rainy season, peaking in September to October, it's wettest at dusk. Rain showers can be torrential and cause flooding, although many are intense but short.

TIME

In winter, Bangkok is 12 hours ahead of EST, 7 hours ahead of the UK, and 6 hours ahead of continental Europe. In summer, it's one hour less.

AVERAGE DAILY MAXIMUM TEMPERATURES

JAN	FEB	MAR	APR	MAY	JUN	JUL	AUG	SEP	OCT	NOV	DEC
83°F	83°F	85°F	86°F	87°F	87°F	86°F	87°F	87°F	86°F	85°F	83°F
28°C	28°C	29°C	30°C	31°C	31°C	30°C	31°C	31°C	30°C	29°C	28°C

Bangkok has three distinct seasons:

Hot season (March to May)—The climate can be unbearable because the high temperatures are intensified by the 90 percent humidity.

Rainy season (June to October)—Hot and humid days are followed by rain, usually at dusk.

Cool season (November to February)—The sky is usually bright and clear; days are reasonably cool and nights pleasantly warm.

WHAT'S ON

January/February
Chinese New Year: Temples are busy, shops close.
Maga Puja: Candle-lit processions at wats for full moon.
March/April *Kite fights and festivals*: On Sanam Luang.
April *Chakri Day* (Apr 6): Celebrates the founding in 1782 of the Chakri dynasty.
Songkran (mid-Apr): The Thai New Year.
May *Royal Plowing Ceremony* (early May): Start of the rice-planting season on Sanam Luang.

Visaka Puja (mid-May): Celebrates the birth, enlightenment and death of the Buddha.
July *Asalha Puja*: Marks Buddha's first sermon and the start of a three-month Rains Retreat.
Bangkok International Film Festival: Shows more than 150 films from around the world.
August *H.M. Queen Sirikit's Birthday* (Aug 12).
September/October
Moon Festival: The Chinese community honors the moon goddess.

October *Ok Pansa*: End of the three-month Rains Retreat. Monks are presented with new robes and gifts.
October/November *Long boat races*.
November *Loy Krathong* (Nov full moon): Small banana-leaf boats with flowers and candles float in celebration of water spirits.
December *New Year's Eve*: Even if it isn't Thai New Year, this can be pretty spectacular in Bangkok. The biggest countdown takes place in front of Central World Square.

Nuneaton Library

Customer ID: *****221

Items that you have renewed

Title: Bangkok
ID: 0143205304
Due: 28 October 2023

Total items: 1
Account balance: £3.70
Borrowed: 1
Overdue: 0
Hold requests: 0
Ready for collection: 0
07/10/2023 11:39

Tel: 0300 555 8171
www.warwickshire.gov.uk/libraries
Follow us on: @warkslibraries
Thank you for visiting Warwickshire Libraries

Bangkok Online

tourismthailand.org
Official site of the Tourism Authority of Thailand with a range of information on Thai art, culture and food, as well as practical information, links to official websites and listings.

richardbarrow.com
Richard Barrow is a British expat who has been living in Thailand for more than 20 years. He blogs and tweets on many issues of interest and use to visitors.

bangkokpost.com
Online offering of the daily *Bangkok Post* with news items, economic reviews, weather reports, restaurant reviews and articles on the capital's sights, culture and art.

bangkok.com
Comprehensive guide to the city's temples, museums, hotels, markets, great shopping and exotic nightlife, as well as tips to make the most of your stay.

thebigchilli.com
Online version of the Bangkok *Big Chilli* magazine with the latest information and listings.

into-asia.com
Easy-to-use site that gives a general insight into Thai language and culture. Useful advice about scams and tourist traps.

bk.asia-city.com
Insider's guide to Bangkok with what's on and reviews of new and old restaurants, nightlife venues and shops.

thailandforvisitors.com
Useful site for planning your visit to the city. It provides information on sights, shopping, accommodations and restaurants and cafés, plus practical tips.

TRAVEL SITE

fodors.com
A complete travel-planning site. You can research prices and weather; reserve air tickets, cars and rooms; ask questions (and get answers) from fellow travelers.

INTERNET ACCESS

The days of having to seek out internet cafés in Bangkok are long gone and the city's hotels, bars, restaurants and other public places are as good as any in offering reliable WiFi connections, more often than not at no charge.

Getting There

VISAS AND TRAVEL INSURANCE

For the latest passport and visa information, go to the United States embassy website at https:/th.usembassy.gov or the British embassy website at gov.uk/government/world/thailand. Check your insurance: It is vital that your travel insurance covers medical expenses, in addition to accidents, trip cancellation, baggage loss and theft. Check the policy covers any continuing treatment for chronic conditions. Keep all receipts in case you need to make a claim.

DON MUEANG AIRPORT

The original international airport, Don Mueang (donmueangairport.com) is now used for domestic flights—do double-check which airport you're traveling through if you're using the capital as a hub. Taxis (stand is located in front of the arrivals hall) operate to, among other destinations, the city center (around 200B) and Suvarnabhumi airport (around 350B0. Buses 554 and 555 serve Suvarnabhumi, and No. 29 goes to central Bangkok (Siam area).

AIRPORTS

Bangkok's main international airport is Suvarnabhumi, located 15 miles (25km) east of downtown Bangkok.

ARRIVING BY AIR

Suvarnabhumi airport (bangkokairportonline.com) is served by excellent transportation links to the city and beyond.

● There is an express bus service (35B) connecting the second floor (gate 5) and the fifth floor (gate 5) of the terminal building with the public transportation center.

● Local bus routes (lines A, B, C, D and L) operate within the airport to connect services, facilities, businesses and offices, including other floors and gates of the passenger terminal, the Novotel Hotel and long-term parking.

● An efficient air rail link operates between Suvarnabhumi and the city center and takes 15–30 minutes. The service connects with the Phaya Thai BTS Skytrain station (which does have a lot of stairs) and the terminal Makkasan station. A single ticket is 45B.

● Airports of Thailand Limited operates 24-hour limousines (aot-limousine.com). The service counter is on the second floor at baggage claim and arrival hall exits, channels A, B and C. Prices vary but expect to pay around 1,500B for a transfer from the airport to the city.

● Taxis operate from the first floor of the passenger terminal (gates 4 and 7). The service

is 24 hours. There are (usually) manned terminals where you collect a ticket showing the number of the lane opposite at which your taxi will pull up. Taxis are metered and prices vary but expect to pay 300B for a journey to the Sukhumvit area. Note that there are two tolls on the main route into the city (one is 25B, the second 50B). Your driver may expect you to pay this rather than add it to your fare so be sure to have some smaller notes on you. Do not use taxis from other sources as these are invariably operated by touts.

● If you have a connecting flight out of Don Mueang airport there is a transfer bus operating between 5am and midnight. It departs from the second floor (gate 3) of the terminal building (if you're arriving from Don Mueang it will drop you on the fourth floor at gate 5). In both directions the service operates hourly between 5am and 10am and from 10pm to midnight and more frequently from 10am to 10pm.

● There are several bus routes from the public transportation center to various parts of Bangkok, but we don't recommend these—see Getting Around ▷ 118–119.

ARRIVING BY TRAIN

Trains from and to Malaysia and Singapore use Hua Lamphong Station, which connects with the MRT subway system which, in turn, connects with the BTS Skytrain at Sala Daeng (two stops away). Or, take a taxi but make sure it's metered or agree a fixed fare.

Getting Around

VISITORS WITH DISABILITIES

Bangkok is particularly difficult for visitors with disabilities—streets are busy with traffic and the river boats hardly stop long enough for anyone to jump on. For information go to dpiap.org, which has some useful resource links. Wheelchair Travel (wheelchairtravel.org) has a section on Bangkok, and tourismthailand.org is useful for the latest news.

BTS SKYTRAIN

The elevated BTS Skytrain (transitbangkok.com) is by far the fastest, coolest and most comfortable way to get around. Trains run every few minutes from 6am to midnight at 15–52B a trip. There are two lines, Silom and Sukhumvit, and neither serves the old city. The only change between lines is at Siam station. The Metro (known as the MRT; transitbangkok.com) has two lines, Blue and Purple, and runs from 6am to midnight. Trains run every 5–10 minutes and the MRT connects with the Skytrain at Asok station. Fares range from 15B to 40B (operated by tokens).

The best way to see the old city is to take the Skytrain to Saphan Taksin and connect with the Chao Phraya River Express Boats (chao-phrayatouristboat.com), which serve piers (*tha*; marked on the fold-out map). Boats are fast and stop at many major sights. A day pass, which can also be bought online, costs 180B. Services run from 9am to 6pm (depending on the departing pier). It's also possible to hire a long-tail boat for a personalized tour of the city's *khlongs* or to a destination of your choice. Prices vary. Ask your hotel concierge or tour operator/guide for advice.

BOATS

Boats not flying any flag will stop at piers where people are waiting to board or passengers are waiting to disembark. Boats flying a yellow or orange flag are express boats that do not stop at every pier. A dark blue flag shows that this is the last one of the day. Special Tourist Boats run between Central Pier and Banglamphu, and the ticket allows you to hop on and off any of these boats.

BUSES

Although there is an extensive bus network, it is not advisable to use them. Aside from it being very difficult to access accurate information on numbers and routes (most information is in Thai), buses are overcrowded, hot and sticky,

and can be a haunt of pickpockets. And with the superb BTS Skytrain and MRT Metro (or the good, old-fashioned *tuk-tuk*), the many alternatives are clean, efficient and safe.

TAXIS

These are usually air-conditioned and metered —check it is switched on. The flag fare is 35B, and stays there for the first 2km (1.5 miles), increasing at roughly 2 baht per km. Expect to pay around 50B for an average journey. Communication can be a challenge, so always carry the name of your hotel or destination written in Thai. Motorcycle taxis are cheaper and faster, but can be dangerous.

Tuk-tuks

Tuk-tuks can be found everywhere in Bangkok and sometimes are useful for short trips if you're in a rush. A ride in an exotic three-wheel *tuk-tuk* "taxi," even the rare one driven in a calm manner, will expose you to traffic fumes and noise to an alarming degree. Two people, three at the very most, can sit comfortably. Having coins helps when paying the fare, which should always be agreed beforehand. Expect to pay from 70B upward for a short journey.

DRIVING

This is definitely not a good idea. In Bangkok the density of traffic and the bewildering mix of traffic directions and lanes—which are subject to constant changes and are rarely signposted in English—make driving very challenging. Car rental at Bangkok's Suvarnabhumi airport is feasible if you are not heading into the city, and expressways, signposted in English, connect the airports with routes to other parts of the country. A non-Thai driver is supposed to show an international driver's license when renting a vehicle, but in practice it is often sufficient to show your national license. Larger fuel stations will accept payment by recognized international credit cards, but in rural areas cash may be required.

ORGANIZED SIGHTSEEING

Bangkok has numerous companies offering tours of all the major sights and attractions. The best and often the most reliable way to start is by consulting your hotel concierge. International company Viator (viator.com) offers a full program in the Thai capital. Excellent regional tour companies like Diethelm (diethelmtravel.com) and Exo Travel (exotravel.com) have a huge choice. Manohra (manohracruises.com) runs river trips on beautifully restored teak rice barges, while Grasshopper Adventures (grasshopperadventures.com) has a great selection of cycling tours.

TOURIST INFORMATION

Association of Thai Travel Agents
✉ Counter at Suvarnabhumi Airport Level 2, Arrivals Hall
🕐 24 hours
Main TAT office
✉ 1600 New Petchaburi Road, Makkasan
☎ 0 2250 5500, tourismthailand.org
🕐 Mon–Fri 8–5

Essential Facts

MONEY MATTERS

- The currency is the Baht (B), divided into 100 satang. Coins are 25 and 50 satang, 1 Baht, 5 Baht and 10 Baht. Notes are 10, 20, 50, 100, 500 and 1,000 Baht.
- Credit cards are widely accepted, although some places may add a surcharge.
- You can withdraw Baht with credit cards from ATMs. If prompted, always choose for the conversion to be charged in the local currency.

EMBASSIES

British Embassy
✉ 14 Thanon Witthaya, Lumphini Pathumwan
☎ 0 2305 8333, gov.uk/government/world/thailand
Canadian Embassy
✉ 15th Floor, Abdulrahim Place, 990 Thanon Rama IV
☎ 0 2636 0540, thailand.gc.ca
Portuguese Embassy
✉ 26 Thanon Charoen Krung, Soi 30
☎ 0 2234 2123, banguecoque.embaixadaportugal.mne.pt
Spanish Embassy
✉ 93/98–99 Lake Rajada Office, Ratchadapisek Road, Klongtoey
☎ 0 2661 8284
US Embassy
✉ 95 Wireless Road
☎ 0 2205 4000, th.usembassy.gov

ELECTRICITY

- 220V, 50-cycle AC. Most hotels have 110V shaver outlets.

EMERGENCIES

- Bangkok is generally safe, but watch for pick-pockets and bag-snatchers in crowded places, especially buses, boats and ferries. Women should take care alone at night.
- Leave valuables and travel documents in your hotel's safety deposit box (leave copies of travel documents at home). Exercise care when dealing with money and credit cards while out and about.
- Take care of credit cards. Keep all receipts and destroy carbons.
- Beware of "bargain" gems, jewelry or other objects, which might later prove to be worthless. Also beware of getting involved in a game of Thai cards as you are sure to lose.
- Beware of taking someone to your room, or of accepting food or drink from strangers, as there have been cases of visitors being drugged and robbed.
- Thais are serious about wanting to stop drug smuggling. Border security is efficient and the maximum penalty is death.

MEDICAL TREATMENT

- All listed hospitals have 24-hour emergency services, but you may need your passport and be asked to pay a deposit. Your medical insurance policy may not be accepted, although major credit cards are.
- Private hospitals: BNH Hospital, 9 Thanon Convent, tel 0 2686 2700; St Louis Hospital, 27 Sathon Tai Road, tel 0 2675 5000.
- Public hospitals: Bumrungrad Hospital, 33 Soi 3 Sukhumvit, tel 0 2066 8888; Samitivej Hospital, 37 Somdet Phra Chao Taksin Road, tel 0 2438 9000.
- Contact your hotel reception first in case of a medical emergency.
- Keep all receipts for claims on your travel insurance when back home.

MEDICINES
● Bangkok is equipped with numerous pharmacies and they are very easy to locate. They are generally extremely well stocked and many drugs and forms of medication are available over the counter.
● Pharmacies are usually open from early morning until late evening, and many pharmacists speak good English.

OPENING HOURS
● Offices: Mon–Fri 8.30–noon, 1–4.30.
● Banks: Mon–Fri 10–3.30.
● Bangkok Bank and exchange counters: daily 7am–8pm (some open to 9pm).
● Shops: Daily 10–6.30 or 7; smaller shops often stay open 12 hours a day. Most shopping centers are open daily 10am–9pm.

POST OFFICES
● The General Post Office (GPO) is at Thanon Charoen Krung (New Road), between the Oriental and Sheraton hotels (open Mon–Fri 8–8, Sat, Sun and holidays 8–1).
● Postage stamps for letters and postcards being sent by airmail are widely available in shops and hotels as well as post offices. Prices vary according to weight and zone.

TELEPHONES
● Although less widely used these days, pre-paid international phone cards are widely available. For extended stays, a local SIM card may be a good option.
● All Thai phone numbers now have eight digits, plus the "0" area code. Always include the "0" when calling within Thailand; omit it if calling from abroad.
● To make an international call from Bangkok, dial 001 or 007, followed by the country code and then the customer number.
● The least expensive way to call internationally is via the internet. WiFi is widely available in Thailand and is free in many hotels, bars, restaurants and public places.

EMERGENCY PHONE NUMBERS
● Ambulance ☎ 1669
● Fire ☎ 199
● Police ☎ 191
● Tourist Assistance Center, tourismthailand.org
● If you are a victim of theft, call the tourist police ☎ 1155

ETIQUETTE
● Thais show great respect for their royal family and religious personalities, as should visitors.
● Women should not touch monks, who also cannot receive offerings directly from them.
● All Buddha images are sacred.
● A public display of anger is taboo.
● Cover arms and legs in temples.
● It is insulting to touch someone's head or back, and it is rude to point toes or the soles of feet at someone or at a Buddha image. Remove shoes upon entering a temple or a private home.
● Thais rarely shake hands, instead placing them together under their chin in a *wai*.

Language

Although English is widely spoken in hotels and restaurants, it is useful to have some Thai. It is quite difficult to get the hang of, as one syllable can be pronounced in five tones, each of which will carry a different meaning. The classic example of this is the syllable *mai*, which, in the different tones, can mean "new," "wood," "burned," "not?" and "not." So *Mái mài mâi mâi mäi* means: "New wood doesn't burn, does it?" Consonants are also pronounced slightly differently. Ask a local Thai to pronounce the words listed below for you in the right tone. And for taxi and *tuk-tuk* drivers, ask someone to write down your destination in Thai script.

THE BASICS	
hello	*sawat-dii krap (man), sawat-dii (woman)*
how are you?	*pen yangai?*
I'm fine	*sabaay dii*
thank you	*khawp khun*
good morning	*sawatdee*
good afternoon/ good evening	*sawadee*
good-bye	*laa gorn*
see you later	*phop gan mai*
sorry, excuse me	*kor toh*
what is your name?	*khun cheu arai?*
my name is…(man)	*phom cheu*
my name is… (woman)	*diichan cheu*
Do you speak English?	*Khun poot pah-sah angkrit dai mai?*
(I) don't understand	*mai khao jai*
yes	*chai*
no	*mai chai*
how do I get to…?	*pai…yng ngai?*
turn right	*lii-o kwaa*
turn left	*lii-o sai*
straight ahead	*dtrong dtrong*
how much?	*thao rai?*
inexpensive	*thuuk*
too expensive	*phaeng pai*
here	*tee-nee*
where	*tee-n*
there	*tee-nan*
when	*muae-rai*

NUMBERS	
0	*suun*
1	*neung*
2	*sawng*
3	*sahm*
4	*sii*
5	*haa*
6	*hok*
7	*jet*
8	*paet*
9	*kao*
10	*sip*
11	*sip-et*
12	*sip-sawng*
20	*yii-sip*
30	*sahm-sip*
100	*neeung roy*

GETTING AROUND

on/to the right	*yoo/bpai taang kwah*
on/to the left	*yoo/bpai taang saai*
opposite	*dtrong-kaam*
straight on	*dtrong bpai*
north	*nuae*
south	*dtai*
east	*dta-wan-ork*
west	*ta-wan-tok*

DAYS/TIME

Monday	*wan jan*
Tuesday	*wan ang-karn*
Wednesday	*wan put*
Thursday	*wanpa-ru-hat-sa-bordee*
Friday	*wan suk*
Saturday	*wan sau*
Sunday	*wan ah-tit*
day	*glang-wan*
today	*wan-nee*
yesterday	*muae-waan-nee*
tomorrow	*wan-prung-nee*

USEFUL WORDS

toilet	*hawng suam*
river	*mae, maee nam lak nam*
restaurant	*raan aahaa*
long-tail boat	*ruea hang yao*
river bank	*rim nam*
hotel	*rohng raem*
train	*rot fai*
bus	*rot meh, rot bat*
taxi	*rot yon*
airport	*sanaam*
station	*sathaanii*
main chapel of a temple	*bot*
pagoda	*chedi*
foreigner	*farang*

MORE USEFUL WORDS

open	*bpert*
closed	*bpit*
entrance	*taang kao*
exit	*taang org*
canal	*khlong*
alley	*soi*
bridge	*sa-paan*
black	*see dam*
white	*see kaow*
bicycle	*rot jak-gra-yarn*
help	*chuoy duoy*
embassy	*sa-taan-toot*
temple	*wat*

MONTHS

January	*mak-ga-rah-kom*
February	*gum-pah-pan*
March	*mee-nah-kom*
April	*may-sah-yon*
May	*pruet-sa-pah-kom*
June	*mi tu nah-yon*
July	*ga-rak-ga-dah-kom*
August	*sing-hah/kom*
September	*gan-yah-yon*
October	*dtu-lah-kom*
November	*pruet-sa-ji-gah-yon*
December	*tan-wah-kom*

Timeline

POLITICAL THAILAND

Thailand has had a some-what turbulent political and democratic track record. Military coups have been common, governments have come and gone with lightning speed, and the military—long an influential and powerful backbone of Thai society—have often "stepped in" when necessary. Occasional incidents of civil unrest and disruption do happen but they have traditionally been confined to small areas of Bangkok. Before you travel, check the latest travel advice with the State Department in the United States (state.gov/travel) or the Foreign and Commonwealth Office in the UK (gov.uk/foreign-travel-advice).

From left: King Chulalongkorn (Rama V) in European dress; portrait of King Chulalongkorn (Rama V); portrait of King Bhumibol Adulyadej (Rama IX), in a decorative frame backed by the national colors and displayed during his birthday celebrations

1530s King Phrajai (ruled 1534–46) re-routes the Chao Phraya River, creating Thonburi on the west bank and Bang Makok on the east.

1825 King Rama III (ruled 1824–51) closes the mouth of the Chao Phraya River to impose isolationist policies and to resist change.

1851 King Rama IV (ruled 1851–68) encourages change and Thailand retains independence during the colonial period.

1868 Rama V (King Chulalongkorn, ruled 1868–1910) continues social reforms.

1932 A bloodless coup replaces absolute monarchy with a constitutional monarchy. King Prajadhipok (Rama VII, ruled 1925–35) abdicates in 1935.

1939 The country's name is changed from Siam to Prathet Thai.

1946 Thailand is admitted to the United Nations. King Bhumibol Adulyadej (King Rama IX) becomes ruling monarch.

2001 Populist Thai Rak Thai party, led by Thaksin Shinawatra, wins power.

2004 On December 26, the Indian Ocean tsunami claims more than 5,000 lives along Thailand's Andaman Coast.

2006 Thaksin is accused of corruption and is overthrown by a military coup, before civilian government is restored in 2007.

2011 The pro-Thaksin Pheu Thai party wins a landslide election victory. Thaksin's sister, Yingluck, becomes prime minister.

2012 Anti-government protesters blockade parliament, fearing a proposed amnesty would enable the return of Thaksin Shinawatra. Police demonstrate in Bangkok and call for the overthrow of prime minister Yingluck Shinawatra.

2014 In February, general elections go ahead but the Constitutional Court declares them invalid. In May, the court orders Yingluck and several ministers out of office. The army seizes power in an August coup and General Prayuth Chan-ocha is made prime minister.

2015 On April 2, King Bhumibol Adulyadej gives his approval for the lifting of martial law.

2016 King Bhumibol Adulyadej dies after 70 years on the throne. There follows a year-long period of mourning.

2017 Crown Prince Maha Vajiralongkorn, King Bhumibol and Queen Sirikit's only son, ascends the throne as Rama X.

2019 Elections to be held designed to end five years of military rule.

WEST MEETS EAST
In the 1960s, the US began building military bases within Thailand to help with the Vietnam War. The needs of the US military brought huge sums of money into Thailand and helped transform Bangkok into the burgeoning modern city it is today.

From left: A traffic police-man wearing a mask; the bronze statue of King Rama VI in Bangkok, in full military uniform; King Maha Vajiralongkorn (Rama X)

Index

CityPack Bangkok

Published by AA Publishing, a trading name of AA Media Limited, whose registered office is Fanum House, Basing View, Basingstoke, Hampshire RG21 4EA. Registered number 06112600.

© **AA Media Limited 2019**

Written by Anthony Sattin and Sylvie Franquet
Updated by David Leck and Anita Sach
Series editor Clare Ashton
Design work Liz Baldin
Colour reprographics Ian Little

Printed and bound in China by 1010 Printing Group Limited

A CIP catalogue record for this book is available from the British Library.

ISBN 978-0-7495-8173-2

The content of this book is believed to be accurate at the time of printing. Due to its nature the content is likely to vary or change and the publisher is not responsible for such change and accordingly is not responsible for the consequences of any reliance by the reader on information that has changed. Any rights that are given to consumers under applicable law are not affected. Opinions expressed are for guidance only and are those of the assessor based on their experience at the time of review and may differ from the reader's opinions based on their subsequent experience.

We have tried to ensure accuracy in this guide, but things do change, so please let us know if you have any comments at travelguides@theAA.com.

A05671
Maps in this title produced from mapping data supplied by Global Mapping, Brackley, UK © Global Mapping and data available from openstreetmap.org © under the Open Database License found at opendatacommons.org
Transport map © Communicarta Ltd, UK

We would like to thank the following photographers, companies and picture libraries for their assistance in the preparation of this book.

All images copyright of AA/J Holmes, except:

4 AA/D Henley; 6cl AAA/R Strange; 6cc AA/D Henley; 6cr AA/D Henley; 6bl AA/R Strange; 6bc AA/D Henley; 7cr AA/D Henley; 10tb Tourism Authority of Thailand; 11tc Tourism Authority of Thailand; 14ctr AA/D Henley; 16bc AA/D Henley; 16b Tourism Authority of Thailand; 17t AA/R Strange; 17tc AA/R Strange; 17b AA/R Strange; 18c AA/D Henley; 18cb The Peninsula Hotel, Bangkok; 19(i) AA/R Strange; 20/21 AA/R Strange; 24l AA/D Henley; 24/5t AA/D Henley; 24/5b Tourism Authority of Thailand; 25cr AA/D Henley; 26/7 Tourism Authority of Thailand; 27tr Tourism Authority of Thailand; 27cr Tourism Authority of Thailand; 28l Tourism Authority of Thailand; 28r Tourism Authority of Thailand; 30l Roger Cracknell22/Thailand/Alamy Stock Photo; 30/1 AA/D Henley; 32 AA/R Strange; 32/3 AA/R Strange; 33 AA/R Strange; 34l AA/R Strange; 34/5t AA/D Henley; 34/5b AA/D Henley; 35cr AA/D Henley; 36 Simon Reddy/Alamy Stock Photo; 36/7 Kerry Dunstone/Alamy Stock Photo; 39r AA/R Strange; 40bl Nunnicha Supagrit/ Alamy; 40br AA/R Strange; 41b AA/R Strange; 45 Tourism Authority of Thailand; 50cl Tourism Authority of Thailand; 52/3 Zoonar GmbH/Alamy Stock Photo; 53 Tim Downs/Alamy Stock Photo; 54l Saranya Wangcharoentak; 54r Saranya Wangcharoentak; 56/7 Tourism Authority of Thailand; 57 Tourism Authority of Thailand; 58br Hemis/Alamy Stock Photo; 59bl Tourism Authority of Thailand; 59br Tourism Authority of Thailand; 72l AA/D Henley; 72tr AA/D Henley; 72cr AA/D Henley; 73 AA/D Henley; 74tl AA/R Strange; 75tl AA/D Henley; 75tr Tourism Authority Thailand; 76/77 travelbild.com/Alamy Stock Photo; 77 AA/D Henley; 78 Stockinasia/Alamy Stock Photo; 80bl Mervyn Rees/Alamy Stock Photo; 81bl Museum of Floral Culture; 93 AA/R Strange; 96/7 Tourism Authority of Thailand; 97t Tourism Authority of Thailand; 97c Tourism Authority of Thailand; 98/9t Tourism Authority of Thailand; 98cl Tourism Authority of Thailand; 98/9c Tourism Authority of Thailand; 99tr AA/D Henley; 99cr AA/D Henley; 102l Prasart Museum; 102c Prasart Museum; 102r Prasart Museum; 103bl Duy Phuong Nguyen/Alamy Stock Photo; 103br AA/D Henley; 104/5t AA/R Strange; 104bl AA/D Henley; 104bc AA/D Henley; 104br AA/R Strange; 105bl Tourism Authority of Thailand; 105blc AA/R Strange; 105bcr AA/D Henley; 105br AAA/R Strange; 106t AA/R Strange; 106bl AA/D Henley; 106bcl AA/D Henley; 106bc AA/D Henley; 106bcr AA/D Henley; 106br AA/D Henley; 108/9t AA/C Sawyer; 108tr AA/D Henley; 108tcr Atlanta Hotel, Bangkok, Oliver Spalt; 108bcr The Peninsula Hotel, Bangkok; 108br AA/J Holmes; 110/1 AA/C Sawyer; 112 AA/C Sawyer; 124bl AA/D Henley; 124br AA/D Henley; 124/5b AA/R Strange; 125bl AA/R Strange; 125bc AA/R Strange; 125br Xinhua/ Alamy Stock Photo

Every effort has been made to trace the copyright holders, and we apologise in advance for any unintentional omissions or errors. We would be pleased to apply any corrections in a following edition of this publication.

Titles in the Series

- Amsterdam
- Bangkok
- Barcelona
- Berlin
- Boston
- Brussels & Bruges
- Budapest
- Dubai
- Dublin
- Edinburgh
- Florence
- Hong Kong
- Istanbul
- Krakow
- Las Vegas
- Lisbon
- London
- Madrid
- Milan
- Munich
- New York
- Orlando
- Paris
- Prague
- Rome
- San Francisco
- Shanghai
- Singapore
- Sydney
- Toronto
- Venice
- Vienna
- Washington